FIG LEAVES ARE NOT ENOUGH

FIG LEAVES
ARE NOT ENOUGH

Open Letters on Modesty in Dress

Dom Pius Mary Noonan, OSB, STD

CANA PRESS

Cana Press © 2024, all rights reserved.
No part of this book may be reproduced or transmitted,
in any form or by any means, without permission.

Cover image: Adam & Eve, detail of a painted
high altar frontal depicting the fall of man.
Photo by Fr Lawrence Lew OP

For information, address:
PO Box 85,
Colebrook,
Tasmania, 7027,
Australia

notredamemonastery.org

ISBN

978-0-9756588-9-5

To All Those Women
Who Now or in the Future
Glorify God and Edify the World
by the Beauty and the Dignity of their Dress,
this Book is Reverently and Gratefully Dedicated

Acknowledgement

This book owes much to the constructive criticism of many women of various ages and walks of life who patiently read through one or more of the numerous drafts of my manuscript and made many useful comments. Even though their modesty prevents them from wanting their names to be made public, I would like to here thank them all from the bottom of my heart. May Mary Immaculate reward them all in abundance! As for any errors or inexactitudes that may still be found in the text, I alone bear the responsibility for them, and beg the reader's forbearance as I treat a highly sensitive but crucial topic.

That in All Things God May be Glorified

Rule of St Benedict, ch. 57

Contents

Acknowledgement vii
Author's Preface xi

FIRST CORRESPONDENCE
The Veil 1
Female Dignity and the Veil 7
The Pauline Precept 9
Weddings 14
The Fundamental Integration of Body and Soul 15

SECOND CORRESPONDENCE
Original Sin: The Spanner in the Works 21
Original Sin 30
Concupiscence 33
Modesty the Guardian of Chastity 36
Modesty as Virtue and Fruit 38
Modesty and the Mutual Attraction of the Sexes 41
Modesty as a Check for Curiosity and
    Custody of the Senses 45
Modesty in Words 48
Modesty in Behaviour 50
The Sin of Immodesty 51

THIRD CORRESPONDENCE
Modesty in the Context of Modern Culture 55
Fashions in History 61
Fashions That Offend God 62
An Out of Place Objection 66
True Beauty 67
The Objective Norm of Modesty 69
The Vessel of Life 72
Heels, Cosmetics and Other Adornments 73

FOURTH CORRESPONDENCE
Modesty in the Practicalities of Daily Modern Life 77
Women and Trousers 83
Differences in Visual Perception 85
Ideological Issues 87
Dignity and Decorum 90
Exceptions 92
Sportswear 94
Swimming Suits 96
A Modest Solution 100
Personal Modesty and Courtesy for Others 102

FINAL EXHORTATION
Urgent Letter of Appeal to All Spiritual Daughters 105

Notes 111

APPENDIX
Practical Points on Modesty for Men and Women 123
Preliminary Consideration 124
Standards for Women 124
Standards for Men 126
Modesty in Church 127

A FINAL THOUGHT
Admonition Against Vanity from St Frances of Rome 129

Author's Preface

For many years now it has been on my mind to write a book on modesty in dress. In that time other books or articles have appeared here and there, giving hope that a true revival of Christian modesty is making its way through the various ranks of our society.

There is a need for it, as the fashions in the west over the past one hundred years have gone from slightly provocative to outright immodest and now to utterly vulgar and ugly. Both modesty and beauty have, in large part, been lost, making for a world that is more and more unpleasant to live in.

One of the things that kept me from writing this book was the thought that it would be best written by a woman. I have the greatest respect for those women who have in recent years courageously done fine work on this topic. However, it also appears to me that a book by a man has some advantages. Although there is a real risk of undergoing criticism for being judgmental, misogynist, obsessed, or any other list of unpleasant qualifiers, there is also a real advantage in having a male perspective on this question. After all, men are the ones who are primarily affected by the way women dress. My words in this book are not theory, but practice.

I am also a priest, and as such receive the confidences of many men and women. I know the problem from the inside as well as from the outside. One of the things I have noticed, however, is that priests have been more and more reluctant to speak to this matter in public. The moral scandals of the clergy have obviously weighed heavily upon many good priests who are fearful of even bringing up the topic, lest they be seen as imbalanced, biased, or worse.

The reality remains, however, that the priest is spiritual father of his faithful. He has duties to them. He must instruct them and, when necessary, admonish them. It is my hope that this little book will be an incentive to many of my brother priests to muster the courage to be outspoken on the question of Christian modesty. So much depends upon it. I am even of the mind that it is a priority. Without it the restoration of a Christian culture is simply not possible.

The book is presented in the form of correspondence between myself and a spiritual daughter whom I call Amanda. She is a real person, though this is not her real name. Amanda (from the Latin verb amare – meaning "she who wants to be loved") was chosen because every woman wants to be loved. Women are God's masterpiece, the very image of the being He made to receive and welcome His love. Women are designed to be the heart of the family, and they are therefore made for love.

It is precisely this desire for love which leads so many women astray, causing them to imagine they will attract men and find love if they reveal their bodies to them. Sadly, they never find love that way. All they find is a base, fleeting passion, that burns out like a match, and dies, often leaving in its wake a heart ravaged by fire. True love is born in the heart of man when he discovers the beauty that a woman hides deep down in the heart of her person created by God and destined to see Him. Paradoxically, that beauty can be found only if it is hidden in mystery. If it is concealed behind modest, dignified and beautiful apparel, it touches what is most noble in man and inspires him to sacrifice all that he has, even his very life, to obtain it, honour it and defend it.

These letters, though not actual historical letters, do reflect correspondence and conversations on these topics over the years, with Amanda but also with many other women and men. Her personal case inspired the particular approach these letters take – which may surprise some –, starting with good, pious women who, though dressing modestly at church and most of the time outside of church, will nevertheless be led every now and then to fail, and sometimes gravely, in modesty. There are many women in this case in our churches, even in traditional circles. Even where church garb is excellent, peer pressure outside leads them on occasion to follow the crowd, even to spiritual disaster. Amanda's evolution and growth in the spiritual life has been amazing. Starting with the veil at Mass, she came to realise the much more vast implications of modesty at all times, and from there she has been led to a very deep and fruitful spiritual life lived for God alone.

My hope is to ultimately reach the legions of women out there who simply are clueless about modesty, many of whom, often through no fault of their own, have fallen prey to the ideology of the cultural revolution and as a result have lost nearly all moral compass in matters of dress and comportment. I feel that Amanda's itinerary can be an inspiration to many of our good women, both young and less young, and they in turn can then go out and convert their sisters, helping them discover God's mercy along with their own true worth, dignity and beauty.

FIRST CORRESPONDENCE

The Veil

Come before Him: worship the Lord in the beauty of holiness.

1 Chronicles 16:29

11 February 2023
Feast of Our Lady of Lourdes

Dear Father,

It was lovely seeing you at the recent retreat after such a long time. I hope you do not mind me writing to you so soon after, but it was my first retreat and I have so many questions that have arisen since. I will however limit myself to one of them here.

Father, I'm sorry if this question might be silly, but it's about wearing a veil in church. As you may remember, where I grew up, most females wore a veil and it is something my sisters and mother have always done. However, when at university, in the church I attend with a lot of young people, many of the girls often speak about "discerning to veil". There are some girls who think that wearing a veil is a sign of pride, and others who feel it comes from an old-fashioned notion having to do with a patriarchal society that oppresses females, and pretty much all of them think it is something that should be discerned. Their attitudes towards girls wearing dresses to church is similar, and some say it does not matter what one wears to church at all, as it is how we are on the inside that counts. It confuses me to the point where I think perhaps I should stop wearing a veil if others do not?

However, this last week at the retreat, spending a lot of time with the Blessed Sacrament made me realise that I should wear a veil no matter which church I attend, for every church is the house of God, and surely it is for Him that we wear a veil and no other reason? But then, that of course made me wonder—does that mean everybody should? And why do women cover their heads, but men do not? As I said, I have no objection to wearing a veil, and actually I much prefer it as I find myself less distracted and less inclined to make eye contact when wearing a veil.

While I agree with the objections of some of my classmates that it is the intention that counts, I find myself uneasy at their suggestion that it does not matter what one wears—I can't but help but notice that when I dress differently, when I do wear a veil, I find that my behaviour is also somewhat influenced. But perhaps this is just me? I hope you manage to understand what I am getting at and I do apologise if it is a bit jumbled.

With sincerest gratitude through Christ,

Amanda

A woman does not acquire a man's dignity by having her head uncovered, but rather loses her own.

St John Chrysostom

25 March 2023
Feast of the Annunciation

Dear Amanda,

Thank you for getting in touch. I am happy to know you had a fruitful retreat. It was nice to see both you and the other members of your family there. It seems just the other day that you and your sister were little toddlers when I used to visit your parents.

Your questions are very pertinent ones. You have made some interesting observations, all of which demonstrate that you have a strong *sensus fidei*,[1] and this is very important in the spiritual life. I offer the following reflections for your consideration.

Female Dignity and the Veil

The first point that occurs to me is that in our Catholic religion, all things holy are veiled. A veil is placed over the chalice, over the ciborium, over the tabernacle. The priest is veiled with sacred vestments when he is at the altar. The nun is veiled when consecrated to God. Veiling is a sign of respect for the dignity of God's presence. A woman does not clothe her body because she is afraid or ashamed of it, but because of its great dignity. It is a mystery, it is precious; it is sacred; it is the temple of the Holy Spirit.

Why are women so special, you might be asking yourself? Like the tabernacle which contains the Bread of Life, a woman is the tabernacle in which God creates new life. Because of this, we can say that the female body is, in a certain sense, more sacred than the male body, for the simple reason that it is capable of bringing to life a new human person created in the image and likeness of God, and destined to see God for all eternity. Reflecting on what he calls this "frightful privilege" of woman, G. K. Chesterton was moved to write, in his habitual provocative and paradoxical style, that considering this attentively, "no one… can quite believe in the equality of the sexes".[2] In passing, I might add that anyone who considers attentively the preeminent role the Catholic Church acknowledges to the Blessed Virgin Mary who conceived in her womb and nursed with her own milk God Himself in the flesh, cannot possibly entertain for a single second the absurd claim that the Church is, or was at any time in her history, a misogynist patriarchy intent on oppressing women.

A second reason for the veil is that if men represent Christ the Bridegroom, women represent His Bride, the Church. As a bride veils herself on the day of her nuptials, so the woman who veils herself in God's holy temple acknowledges that she symbolises the Church, and thereby implicitly asks Christ to enter into her heart to make her spiritually fecund by means of His grace. At the same time and for the same reason, by wearing a veil, a woman proclaims that men and women are not interchangeable. She acknowledges the God-given complementarity of man and woman, created in the image of God.

Thirdly, wearing the veil is a way of dressing up for God; it tells Him how honoured the woman feels to be able to enter His house to pray, and manifests her humility and submission before Him, thus drawing down His graces and blessings upon her and those she prays for. It contributes to her beauty and helps her and everyone else honour God in much the same way that we only offer to God precious and beautiful vestments, sacred vessels and architecture. All contributes to giving God the worship that is due to Him. A woman who would be invited to Buckingham Palace to meet the King or to the White House to meet the President would wear her absolute finest apparel. To this day, famous women, even non-Catholics, adhere to the dress code of wearing a veil to meet the Pope. How much more should this be the case when going to the House of God and approaching the sacred altar where God Himself is present?

Fourthly, by wearing a veil in church a woman imitates Mary, who is always veiled in her apparitions. Our Lady is the true Ark of the Covenant in which God united Himself with human nature. By imitating the Mother of God, a woman is asking God to effectively fill her with His grace so that she can be an instrument of grace for others.

A fifth reason is that veiling helps a woman to pray. Just as the priest, in the traditional Mass, comes to the altar with his head covered as a sign of recollectedness, so women are helped to pray with fewer distractions and greater recollectedness when they wear the veil.

A sixth is that when women wear a veil in church, they also help men to pray, for the veil protects, safeguards and exalts the natural beauty of woman, inspiring men with awe and respect for her dignity, and barring their natural curiosity to see more of her.

The Pauline Precept

There is a seventh and preponderant motive for which the veil should be worn, and that is the formal precept of the apostle St Paul, from which followed a universal custom in the Church. Let's read the somewhat long passage in which the apostle explains himself. It holds many valuable lessons for us:

> *Be ye followers of me, as I also am of Christ. Now I praise you, brethren, that in all things you are mindful of me: and keep my ordinances as I have delivered them to you. But I would have you know, that the head of every man is Christ; and the head of the woman is the man; and the head of Christ is God. Every man praying or prophesying with his head covered, disgraceth his head. But every woman praying or prophesying with her head not covered, disgraceth her head: for it is all one as if she were shaven. For if a woman be not covered, let her be shorn. But if it*

be a shame to a woman to be shorn or made bald, let her cover her head. The man indeed ought not to cover his head, because he is the image and glory of God; but the woman is the glory of the man. For the man is not of the woman, but the woman of the man. For the man was not created for the woman, but the woman for the man. Therefore ought the woman to have a power over her head, because of the angels. But yet neither is the man without the woman, nor the woman without the man, in the Lord. For as the woman is of the man, so also is the man by the woman: but all things of God. You yourselves judge: doth it become a woman, to pray unto God uncovered? Doth not even nature itself teach you, that a man indeed, if he nourish his hair, it is a shame unto him? But if a woman nourish her hair, it is a glory to her; for her hair is given to her for a covering. But if any man seem to be contentious, we have no such custom, nor the Church of God.[3]

The opening words of this passage make it clear that the apostle did not invent the practice of veiling, but was only handing on the custom received from those before him, and ultimately no doubt, from the Synagogue. The final words, however, make clear that this practice has never been without its contradictors. There may be plenty of reasons for not liking it, but the apostle is affirming that being contentious of ancient customs is simply not the Christian way. A true Christian respects what has been handed down from antiquity, even if he/she does not fully understand it, agree with it, or for that matter, like it. St Paul clearly leaves no room for any kind of discernment.

Furthermore, following upon the apostolic command, the local laws around Christendom prescribed the wearing of the veil in churches,[4] and this was sanctioned universally in the 1917 Code of Canon Law. In the 1960's in the wake of the Second Vatican Council when so many changes affected the Church, the custom was left aside in most places, even though there is not a single ecclesiastical decree that one can point to as dispensing from the obligation to wear the veil.[5] Indeed, how could there be? The Church cannot contradict Holy Scripture and apostolic teaching that is presented in such a clear way. Times and customs may change, but God's laws never change or become outdated. So, what we must say is that the custom was set aside and lost in most places, with, sadly, virtually no resistance from the clergy. I must, however, insist that the failure of the clergy to enforce the veil is certainly not sufficient for the obligation to no longer exist, given the clarity of the apostle's witness. It only means that the clergy did not stand up for the defence of the tradition, perhaps out of a misguided concern for the role of the laity and a rash cave-in to feminism, for which they will have to answer to God.

You will find those who say that St Paul's prescription was just a cultural taboo that the Church accepted, but this fits neither the data of history nor the text of the epistle. Even though St Paul refers to attitudes that he says are grounded in nature (*Doth not even nature itself teach you, that a man indeed, if he nourish his hair, it is a shame unto him? But if a woman nourish her hair, it is a glory to her; for her hair is given to her for a covering*), he bases his teaching on *tradition*, that is to say, what was handed down, not by cultural custom, but by apostolic, and therefore, divine teaching. It has literally nothing to do with cultural usage; it is a religious gesture, and therefore one that abides as long as does the Church of Christ.

This being so, if we want to come to a better understanding of what St Paul is saying, we have to look for theological reasons. The whole question really revolves around the Greek word *exousia* (in Latin, *potestas*) which literally means *power* or *authority,* which the apostle says the woman must have over her head, and which is symbolised by the veil.

Now, there are at least two ways of reading that text. It seems primarily to mean that the veil over her head symbolises that woman is under an authority, that of her husband.

From this point of view, the veil stresses the God-given ordered hierarchy of marriage in which, as Pius XI said so eloquently in the encyclical *Casti Connubii*, the husband is the head of the family and the wife is the heart. No one will contest that the head is above the heart, but neither will they admit that the head is more important than the heart. Both are essential; both have their irreplaceable and non-interchangeable roles.

So, if we interpret it this way, what St Paul is saying is that, by wearing a veil in church, the woman is professing openly her belief that all things are ordered by God according to His wisdom, and if her husband has the primacy of authority in the household, she, and she alone, has the primacy of love; she is the living heart of the family. We may also add to this another consideration found in St Paul's epistle to the Ephesians,[6] where he compares the husband to Christ and the wife to the Church. Just as the Church is under the authority of Christ, but is part of His Body and has been given a share in His divinity, so the wife is under her husband, being an essential part of his body, and on equal footing of dignity with him, even though her role is distinct from his. So, we have here a very beautiful profession of faith in the order of the universe, without which nothing can function properly.

That mention of order and authority leads to other possible considerations on the "power" over the woman's head. Here it can be likened to the crown on the head of a queen. The crown symbolises that the queen has a very special and unique power or authority. So the woman, by wearing the veil, professes that she has, and she is conscious of the fact that she has, very real authority in the household. There, she is truly a queen to be respected and honoured.

This interpretation seems to be confirmed by the addition of the words: "because of the angels". Even though some commentators say that St Paul is here referring to the clergy who are present in church presiding over the ceremonies—and according to this, it would mean that the woman must cover her head in order to avoid giving distractions to the priests, for yes, the priest, like any man, can be distracted when he sees a beautiful woman—, it is also possible to see here an allusion to the order of the universe of which the angels are an essential part. The angels were created in the nine hierarchical choirs, and because of that, they are supremely devoted to maintaining rank, for rank is of God and it allows every creature to prosper in its place. So, when St Paul says the woman should veil herself because of the angels, he is essentially saying that by veiling herself she is giving everyone a visible witness to the hierarchical structure and order of the universe in which all things flow from God and are ordered back to Him.

This brings up another very important point, Amanda, which I invite you to consider very carefully. If we do understand by "angels" the priest and other sacred ministers, by wearing the veil at Mass you are being a very great help and edification to them. There is one obvious reason, already mentioned, in that the feminine beauty of either your hair or face will not be a distraction for them if you are veiled. But there is another, much deeper reason. By wearing the veil, you manifest authority: yours, that of your husband (if and when you have one), and thereby that of all God's children. So when the priest sees a veiled woman at Mass, he sees a soul respectful of the God-given order of things. And since the priest too is one of the faithful, he actually sees in her an image of himself, in submission to God, and that reminds him of the devotion and obedience he must have to the Creator of all things. When a priest sees the veil, in other words, he sees the Church in submission to Christ, and he is reminded that he too is part of that Church, and therefore that he too owes submission to Christ, in particular by accepting the revealed dogma and Tradition and all that goes with it, instead of trying to remake the Church in his own image, as we see, sadly, many clergy doing today.

Finally, when a priest gives Holy Communion to a modestly clothed woman wearing the veil, he beholds an image of the soul that humbles herself before God, and God, acknowledging her humility, deigns to fill her with His divinity. We could apply here the marvellous words of St Elizabeth of the Trinity: "It is in the very depths that the divine impact takes place, where the abyss of our nothingness encounters the Abyss of mercy, the immensity of the all of God".[7]

There is so much to learn from the veil, and so much is lost when the veil is lost!

Weddings

On this topic of female attire in churches, Amanda, I would like to say a word on weddings. Weddings are no exception to the rule of modesty. If you are ever part of a bridal party (or when you yourself get married), a bride and her bridesmaids have the grave obligation to wear very modest dresses. It seems to still be the custom in most places for the bride to wear a veil, but sadly the gowns are, more often than not, dreadfully immodest, strapless, with exposed shoulders, plunging necklines, backless, or even of transparent fabric. Now I understand, that these brides and their attendants are simply wanting to look beautiful and special and likely to have no ill intention, but this is no justification for being gravely immodest and attracting undue attention to their bodies. A bride and her attendants must not stand at the altar attired in such a way, for by doing so, they not only jeopardise the blessing of God that they are asking through the Church on such an important day, they are actually an occasion of sin—that is to say a scandal, which means a stumbling block that may cause others to fall—to all the men present in the church, including the priest. They can also be a scandal for the children, especially the young girls who are present, who, when they become adults, will always be inclined to imitate later what they see on such occasions. Due to the sacredness of the place, it is hard not to qualify such wantonness as sacrilegious.[8]

By the way, do you know why a bride wears a veil to her wedding? The veil, which traditionally covers the face as well as the hair and shoulders, and is lifted by the Bridegroom, was so that no one but he could see her beauty. By means of the veil, she says effectively to her husband: I am for your eyes only. So what sense can it possibly make for a bride to wear a veil and at the same time exhibit before all the men present her shoulders, back and even part of her breasts? We are in the realm of the sacrilegiously absurd.

Given all this, it should be clear that weddings are no exception to the rule of modesty, neither for the bride, nor for any of the women involved in the wedding, all the more since they are so visible to the congregation. Here again, the clergy have a grave responsibility before God.[9] The moral authority given to a priest by the Church is precisely for the admonishing and guardianship of souls so that they may be led to Christ. Therefore, it is the priest's duty (and only his) to charitably enlighten and gently admonish those men and women who are dressed in attire not fitting for the due worship of God. These souls are under his care, and if he fails in this regard, he will have to answer to God.[10]

The Fundamental Integration of Body and Soul

Amanda, the modesty of your apparel, whether at church or in your daily life, should be consistent. It should not change in any context, for the simple reason that it is intimately dependent upon an unchanging reality: the fundamental connection between body and soul, the interaction between internals and externals. You alluded quite correctly in your letter to the fact that you act differently when dressed differently. This is not your imagination playing tricks on you; there is a reason for it.

The definition of a human being is the intricate union of body (the material part) and soul (the immaterial, spiritual, immortal part). The body we have in common with animals, but the immortal soul that is able to choose between good and evil is exclusive to human beings. Soul and body, though distinct, are not separate; they are both essential parts of our human nature, that are fundamentally integrated in order to function as a living human being. While the soul gives life and motion to the body, the body in turn is required, in this life, for the proper functioning of the soul. Another way of putting it is that the soul animates the body and the body influences the soul.

A crucial consequence of this is that, if the soul wants to grow in virtue, which is essentially a habit of goodness which produces good fruit, the soul cannot be content with just thinking about or even desiring virtue or goodness; thoughts and desires must be followed up by actions which can only be carried out by the body. So when you perform actions with your body that are ordered towards the good, your soul grows in the accompanying virtues. The virtues adorn your soul like precious jewels adorn a crown and, on a practical level, help you excel in still other virtues. Likewise, bad actions create bad habits called vices which disfigure the original plan God had for your soul.

These are not just pious allegories. Growth in virtue is a reality that is imprinted on the soul. If you wish to grow and become strong in virtues such as modesty, prudence, chastity, etc. and find it easier to practice virtue, you have at your finger tips the means of doing so, namely, performing the acts of those virtues. Therefore, the way we act with our body has a direct effect on our soul, and vice versa. Sadly, modern idealism has led many to imagine that all that matters is what they think with their minds, and so it doesn't make any difference what they do with their bodies. This is false; it is a devastating error that has left so much spiritual ruin in the landscape of our modern world. What we do with our bodies shapes our very soul and makes it either good or bad, virtuous or vicious.

For example, when we kneel, bow or make the sign of the cross, these external signs and gestures, when fostered in a proper way, prepare internal changes that form internal dispositions in our soul. When a person tells lies or cheats or performs acts of impurity, they *become* a liar, a cheater, impure. The more one completes good or bad actions, the easier the good or bad actions become to perform: in this way a person *becomes* good or *becomes* evil. The same goes for every virtue including that of modesty, where the accompanying action is essentially the way we choose to dress. At the end of the day, if you dress modestly, you *become* modest and chaste. If you dress immodestly, you *become* immodest and unchaste.

Have you ever noticed how it is that priests and nuns, who wear cassocks or habits, command a certain dignity and impose respect in those who see them? They have given their lives to God, and their habit reveals that to anyone who sees them. They "speak" of God just by the way they dress. In turn, this apparel inclines them to act in a certain way and to avoid certain activities and places, simply because their dress imposes upon them the dignity of their position. If they "kick the habit" and begin to dress like the laity, behaviours often change, because they no longer have that constant reminder of their being consecrated to God.

In the same way, it is no secret that women are inclined to act differently depending on the way they dress. If they wear jeans, t-shirt and sneakers, they tend to conduct themselves in a commonplace, undignified manner. When they have a beautiful dress on, they are more likely to bear themselves in a graceful, demure manner. The reason for this is that the nature of the clothing forces the person to move differently according to how the item is made. The effect of feminine apparel, however, will not just extend to how you move around; it will slowly extend to much of your external interactions as well as internal attitudes. Many women have been surprised when experiencing this change within themselves that follows upon dressing with dignity.

One of the strikingly sad things that one notices when studying the evolution of fashions over the past century is that in the early years after World War I, and then especially after World War II, the fashions remained feminine but became increasingly immodest: the hems got higher and higher and the necklines tended to lower, shoulders were uncovered, the form of the body was more and more pronounced, etc. But gradually, from the 1960's, women tended to dress more and more like men do, thus losing the prerogative of beauty, until today when we see the fashions actually making them more and more ugly with, for example, worn-out jeans with holes in the knees (or even the thighs...), tattoos that disfigure their arms and legs, nose-rings, lip-rings, tongue-rings....

Knowing what you do now, Amanda, about the interaction between body and soul, I do hope you begin to seriously consider how a change in external dress inevitably leads to a change in mentality... If a woman begins to dress like a man, she will, even if she does not intend to, slowly start to adopt masculine mannerisms and habits. At the very least, the polarity of gender is reduced, and the world loses the beautiful complementarity of the sexes.

The revolution inaugurated by immodesty in dress will not stop until its ultimate consequences are before us. The push for moral licentiousness through immodesty in dress was already gaining momentum in the 18th century and had as its ultimate goal to make public nudity acceptable. This was clearly demonstrated when at the height of the French revolution, on December 10, 1793, an angry mob rushed into the Cathedral of Notre Dame in Paris, seized the statue of the Virgin Most Pure, and sacrilegiously dashed it to the floor. Thereupon, as a symbol of the nudist program of licentiousness and feminine emancipation, they enthroned in Mary's place on the altar a nude woman, the "goddess of reason." The nudist banner of rebellion against the Church's teaching on modesty was raised high on this occasion, inviting Catholic women to enlist under it. Two centuries later we see it all playing out before us. This makes it clear that by the undue exhibition of flesh, a woman is, whatever her intentions might be, playing the goddess. And that is sacrilegious. The reality is that feminine beauty is one of God's gifts to the world, and women have the prerogative and the duty to make it shine brighter. But in order for that beauty to edify men and not be a stumbling block to them, it must be veiled by modest clothing. Such is the teaching of nature, such is the teaching of the Church handed down by Tradition.

I hope the above have clarified your questions. Perhaps you might try to put it into practice to see for yourself how the way you dress influences not only the way you move around, but also the way others interact with you. Try to wear only dresses for a month and always wear a veil to church. See if you feel and behave differently. Mind you, the dress does not need to be ostentatious—indeed, it should not!—, but feminine and dignified, with simplicity and modesty; beautiful, but not distracting others by any undue revealing of your beauty. I repeat, Amanda: look feminine and beautiful, not cheap and vulgar! The world so needs it.

Please keep me in your prayers, and rest assured of mine for you.

Your Father in Christ

SECOND CORRESPONDENCE

Original Sin:
The Spanner in the Works

*The Lord God made for Adam and his wife,
garments of skins, and clothed them.*

Genesis 3:21

1 May 2023
Month of Mary

Dear Father,

Thank you so much for taking the time to write such a detailed reply. Your letter made perfect sense and gave me so much food for thought. One thing that really hit home was the connection between the soul and the body and how they are so interconnected and one affects the other. It is something I have never thought about or even considered.

So, I did put into practice some of the suggestions you made in your last letter. I have always dressed up for church, because I thought it was the right thing to do. However, I always thought it was OK to dress differently (like everybody else!) in my everyday life.

Since getting back from retreat I have been trying to keep up with a bit of a regular prayer life and have been trying to visit the Blessed Sacrament during the week while I am at university and also say the Rosary daily. I noticed that because I was wearing a dress and a veil for these visits, it often meant that most of my week, even when attending classes, I was in more feminine attire. I was surprised that I did feel very different to how I was normally dressed and noticed that even small mannerisms or actions changed (one must move differently while wearing a dress and a skirt than in trousers or shorts!).

Father, the month did go well. However, I feel very ashamed about something that happened towards its end. No doubt it is bothering me so much because what I experienced on this particular occasion is so contrasted with what I described above. I was hesitant in asking you this question, but it is really weighing on my mind and I hope you might be able to enlighten me on what happened that night, as I am still very confused about both my actions as well as the guilt I felt afterwards.

Last week, I attended the 21st birthday party of a close friend. A few weeks ago, some university friends had bought me a dress which I probably would not have usually worn, but I thought because it was a gift from friends, and they were all going to be there, I would wear it to this party. It was a bright yellow strapless, mini-length dress. I'm sorry to go into so much detail Father, but it is mainly because I want to be completely honest in the description so you can then answer the specific question I have. When I looked at myself in the mirror before leaving home, I thought to myself that I looked so different, and for a fleeting moment, I felt that perhaps I should change as I wasn't quite comfortable. However, a friend that was with me told me the dress really suited me and so I decided it was OK, because surely everyone would be dressed similarly. I told myself: when in Rome do as the Romans do, right? I'd also seen other girls from church dressed in similar dresses before, so thought it would be fine.

Well, to be completely honest, Father, I felt extremely uncomfortable. Like I was on show for everyone to look at—and they did, especially the males! I received a lot of very forward compliments and attention. However, the way the men were looking at me made me feel very uncomfortable, as it was a bit too intimate for my liking. I'm ashamed to say that rather than questioning this doubt, I instead had a couple of drinks of alcohol as I thought perhaps it was just my nerves that needed to calm down, but this only made it worse! I felt awful. I wasn't sure why, as everyone else around me seemed to be so comfortable wearing the same clothes and having a good time, but I was quite miserable and wanted to go home.

Father, I remember you telling me once a few years ago to dress always in a way that would find favour with the Mother of God. I fear I let her down terribly that night. When I came home, I remembered a few of the examination of conscience questions for the General Confession on retreat and realised perhaps I had committed a sin and that is why I felt so bad. I thought the male attention would have been something I would like, but I did not feel comfortable with that sort of attention at all. Did I commit a mortal sin, Father? I think I will go to confession as it might be some time before I hear from you, just in case.

I think I will also maybe reduce the time I am spending at church during the week, as I do not feel it is right to go after how I acted this last week.

I hate to trouble you with this, dear Father, for I know you have so much to do, but I am very grateful for allowing me to clarify my doubts with you.

With gratitude for your time, through Christ,

Amanda

**What is it all for?
If they only knew what eternity is.**

*St Jacinta Marto of Fatima, age 9, on seeing
immodest and fashionably dressed women*

24 May 2023
Mary Help of Christians

Dear Amanda,

I am very glad that what I wrote was helpful to you. And I am also very pleased to see that you did put my suggestions into practice and noticed the difference. Before I come to answer your specific questions, let me expand a bit on some of the things that were only implicit in my last letter to you. They will help us understand what went wrong on that night you mention.

Did you ever wonder why it is that we wear clothes to begin with? To protect our bodies from cold and wind and sun, right? Yes, but we also wear them when the weather is perfect and we do not need to protect ourselves from it. Why do you think that is? It is because there is another important reason, which is actually the first reason: clothing safeguards modesty. Modesty (from the Latin word *modus* which means *due order* based on who we are) is a virtue that dictates a certain way of dress and deportment which implements propriety by maintaining a due order in all things. Modesty is meant to safeguard this pearl of great price which is purity, that is to say, the virtue of chastity.

Clothing therefore protects and helps us maintain modesty, which in turn protects chastity and thereby allows behaviour to be in conformity with the true dignity of a human being made in the image and likeness of God. But, of course, there are various kinds of clothing that cover more or less of the body. How does one know how much to cover? Why don't we just cover the bare minimum, those parts that distinguish us as male and female, and which every human instinctively hides from others?

Remember how we spoke of the unity of body and soul? Well, this essential concept underpins all the guidelines of Christian modesty. If you come to grasp the fundamental reason for human frailty, you will then more clearly understand what happened at that party you attended and why you felt so bad. In a nutshell it can be traced back to Original Sin, the sin of our first parents Adam and Eve, and how that sin has left a permanent wound in our human nature.

Original Sin

To understand Original Sin, we must go back to the beginning. When Adam and Eve were created, they were in the state of grace. They had intimate friendship with God. God loved them and delighted to spend time with them. They were His masterpiece, and all of creation was there to serve them. They had perfect bodies free of disease or decay, crystal clear intellects, and passions that were completely subordinate to reason. They had no need of clothing, for the climate in the garden of Paradise included the perfect temperature, nothing to fear from sun, wind or rain, and no objectifying gazing from others.

In addition to all these natural gifts, Adam and Eve also had what are called preternatural gifts. These are gifts that were not due to our nature as such, but were added to it by God who is so generous. These preternatural gifts, which were destined to be passed on to all future generations of the human race if our first parents had not sinned, were the following: *immortality* (they were not to die), *infused knowledge* (knowledge of all natural sciences to a degree that would make the geniuses of history look like little schoolboys); and *immunity from concupiscence.* This immunity means that their reason had such a command over the natural inclinations of the flesh that their appetites were completely ordered and they would always act according to reason. This immunity from concupiscence is almost impossible for us to imagine now, as we are all wounded by Original Sin. Many people cannot imagine eating food solely to be nourished (as opposed to eating because we are craving a favourite particular food). However, for Adam and Eve, before Original Sin, this was a reality. Instead of appetite leading reason, it was reason that would lead the appetite in order to achieve the desired end of nutrition (food) or procreation (intercourse).

You know the story of the Fall, how Satan, under the guise the serpent, tempted Eve, who then tempted Adam. They both disobeyed God's clear command. That is the first, or Original Sin of humanity. Because of this sin, this turning away from God and towards the creature, Adam and Eve not only lost the initial state of innocence, holiness and bliss in which they were created, but nature, which was meant to serve them, turned against them, because they had first turned against God and distorted creation. Since then, the human intellect has been darkened. The will, which was designed to love and serve God and help neighbour, has been weakened and easily turns against God and against fellow humans. Furthermore, Adam and Eve lost entirely the preternatural gifts: now they had to learn everything (having lost infused knowledge), they had to die (having lost immortality) and they had to deal with disordered desires (loss of immunity from concupiscence). This fundamental refusal of God has since perpetuated down through the centuries in all forms of sin.

Sometimes people think Adam and Eve were just like us; poor Eve ate the apple because she was hungry, and God was just cruel to throw them out of paradise for that. Perhaps you yourself have sometimes thought this. It is very important to understand that the punishment which followed upon Original Sin was not cruel, nor was it unfair, but perfectly just. You see, Adam and Eve, with their superior intellects and infused knowledge, knowingly committed that sin and knew the consequences. They knew that God sustained their life and every action, and that without God, they could not even exist. They knew that to disobey God and eat the fruit would be a mortal sin, that is, give death to the soul and separate them from God. And yet, with full knowledge of this, they chose to slap God in the face. They knew that, by this act, they were turning the order of creation upside down, that they were deliberately turning away from God. Adam, as head of the human race, had a particular guilt in this sin. By consenting to put Eve's suggestion above God's formal command, he knowingly wounded the human nature of which he was the head and the source, and he was fully aware that the wound would pass to each and every human being. This is essentially what Original Sin was: a revolt against God by Adam and Eve, with full knowledge of all its consequences.

Since then, all human beings are conceived and born in a state of sin. The human nature Adam and Eve passed on to all their descendants carries with it that grave wound of soul and body. It is very much like how an alcoholic parent will pass on a profound susceptibility to alcoholism to their child at a level that is at once biological, physiological and psychological, and since body and soul are united in the one human nature, this often predisposes the child to be prone to inclinations that may give rise to certain vices (such as intemperance) which can then affect them on a spiritual level. The child of alcoholic parents will not automatically become an alcoholic; his/her free will remains, but the tendency will be there and it will require much effort and struggle to not succumb and remain temperate.

This predisposition of the child is ultimately the consequence of Original Sin, which affects both body and soul, and it is the state into which we are all conceived and born. Fortunately, God, through His infinite mercy, provides a remedy that has raised man spiritually, even higher than Adam and Eve. It was given in the person of Jesus Christ Our Lord. Through baptism in the Name of the Holy Trinity, Original Sin is remitted and we become true children of God. Although the consequences of Original Sin—ignorance, concupiscence and death—will always remain, they can be surmounted. Constant fidelity to grace, especially the grace received through the Sacraments of Confession and Holy Communion, will fortify us, both body and soul, to conquer temptations and win the eternal crown in Heaven.

Concupiscence

Let us now consider what happened after the first sin, for the history gives us the answer to so many questions that many people find themselves asking: If God created us with no clothes, why should we cover up? If God is omnipotent and omniscient, why would He create us to be sexually attracted and not expect us to act on that impulse and use that pleasure on demand? Why are we so easily aroused sexually if He didn't want us to be using our sexual organs every time we have a desire to? The answer to those questions is given in the biblical account.

Do you remember the first thing that happened to Adam and Eve after their sin? *The eyes of them both were opened: and they perceived themselves to be naked.*[11] In other words, as soon as they sinned and turned away from God, even before any change in the weather which would have forced them to find clothes in order to survive, they lost the mastery God had given them over their passions. The flesh now has its demands that go contrary to reason; other humans, intended by God to be loving companions and helpers to be respected as persons, have become objects of conquest and exploitation. Since that day, men are inclined to take advantage of a woman's desire for love and acquire pleasure at her expense, for men are attracted by the pleasure they can get from seeing and touching the female body. Women on the other hand, in order to gratify their desire to be loved, can prey upon the male desire for visual stimulation in such a way that attracts them. Sadly, not a few men prey on feminine beauty instead of admiring, respecting and protecting it, and not a few women use the seductive charm of their beauty to get what they want from men instead of properly, gently and chastely holding sway over men's affections as they were meant to in God's plan. Henceforward, the original naturally good functions of both men and woman are easily subverted and used in the power of sin. This is why we cannot overly stress the tragic event that took place at the beginning of our history. The knowledge of this simple truth casts an amazing light on the mystery of the battle we must all wage for sexual purity. As G. K. Chesterton wrote, Original Sin is "the only part of Christian theology which can really be proved", meaning that it is all too evident![12]

By concupiscence (or disorderly desire) then, we mean that our senses are inclined to seek pleasure in an inordinate way. Before the Fall, our first parents had no concupiscence. Their bodies were the same as ours, but the lower part of the soul which commands the passions was kept in check by the higher part which was fully submissive to God and His will. When Adam and Eve sinned, they thereby broke their bond of communion with God, and instantaneously the flesh revolted against the spirit; this is the meaning of their eyes were opened and *they knew they were naked*.[13]

Before the Fall they knew they were naked as well, but because of the command that the soul had over the body, the latter could not revolt against the spirit; it was kept in check at all times, and therefore there was nothing to be ashamed of. After sin, however, Adam and Eve lose this control; the lower passions seek to be autonomous and are no longer easily held by reason; thus it is that they realise they need to clothe their bodies to avoid the excessive sensual preoccupation which would otherwise lead them down a path that is sub-human, because it resembles that of the animal world in which there is no resistance possible to the sex urge when it presents itself.

I hope you understand now a little more clearly, Amanda, that the events of the night of that party, right from your choice to wear that immodest dress, despite your conscience pricking you, to the reactions of those present, can all be traced back to Original Sin and concupiscence. It was precisely this reaction of concupiscence in your male counterparts that night that led you to feel that you were "on show". A woman, when not modestly dressed, can trigger in a man concupiscence, which is really animal instinct, and is essentially a desire to enjoy a physical pleasure that is contrary to what his reason tells him.

The account of Genesis goes on to tell us what Adam and Eve did when they realised they were naked: they *sewed together fig leaves, and made themselves aprons*.[14] Fig leaves are pretty big leaves compared to other trees, but they are small compared to the size of the human body. The obvious meaning is that they covered the bare minimum. This was understandable. They did not yet know how to make clothes, and so they did the best they could as fast as they could and with what they had at hand; they simply could not bear to remain naked in each other's presence, because they no longer controlled the movements of their flesh.

What is even more significant is that God did not leave them to their own devices. Genesis explicitly tells us that He Himself gave them clothes. *The Lord God made for Adam and his wife, garments of skins, and clothed them.*[15] In other words, God decided that the fig leaves were not enough. It was not enough to cover the bare minimum, to wear a loincloth (a mini-skirt?); one needs more, and the more takes the form of a garment of skin, in other words, a tunic (or dress) that hides not only the skin but also the shape of the body. God did not make them shorts or trousers, but a tunic that veils both flesh and form. These tunics were for both Adam and Eve, for modesty concerns men as well as women. However, because of the natural differences in the sexes, women are far more prone to be treated with less dignity or respect by men than men by women. As St Peter says, they are "the weaker vessel",[16] who can easily become the prey of man, and therefore an occasion of sin for him. Modest dress does much to overcome this.

So, Amanda, hopefully you can now understand a little of why human beings struggle with immoderation in almost all areas that pertain to the flesh. So this now brings us to a further, more general consideration, that of Chastity.

Modesty the Guardian of Chastity

Chastity is part of the cardinal virtue of temperance. As St Thomas points out following Aristotle, the word itself takes its name from the fact that reason "chastises" concupiscence, which, like a child, needs to be disciplined.[17] Chastity is a "moral virtue which leads us to abstain from disordered desire or disordered use of the sexual faculties".[18] Indeed, human sexuality is God-given. Through it, God gives parents to take part in the act of creation itself, an act which only God can perform. This is why we call it "procreation", a word which alludes to the great mystery of human sexuality and its purpose in God's plan, which is to populate Heaven with human beings.

Chastity is precisely the virtue that allows us to approach with serenity the mystery of our sexuality and to ensure that in its practice we are led by reason, not impulse. The sex urge being, along with the instinct of preservation, the most powerful instinct we have, it is clear that the virtue of chastity is going to play a very important role in the development, not only of the individual, but also of the family and of society in general.

So how are chastity and modesty related? Just as modesty should guide our external behaviour with proper decorum—the way we dress, sit, stand, walk, talk, in a word, all our actions—so it is that modesty is the guardian of chastity in all our thoughts, words and deeds. St Thomas says that while chastity helps regulate the most difficult things (the powerful passions and strong desires for pleasure, whose proper end is procreation), modesty regulates that of the easier things, the remote and proximate occasions that may then lead to unholy desires.[19] It is modesty that foresees threatening danger, forbids us to expose ourselves to risk, and demands the avoidance of those occasions.

The situation that you experienced on the night of that party was a lesson in the importance of modesty and how it safeguards chastity. I will expand on this in more detail below, but briefly for now, I hope you realise that when you made the choice of wearing that dress, you made the choice of putting aside modesty. When modesty was put aside in dress, immoderation in other behaviours will easily follow (in this situation, it was the drinking of alcohol to silence the voice of reason and conscience). When modesty is weakened, unchaste words, deeds and actions are invited in freely. Even though, from what you have described, you did not have a malicious intention, the putting aside of modesty then prompted the unchaste looks from the opposite sex. It is for this reason that you felt so vulnerable and uncomfortable, because the admiration you were gaining was more than likely originating from the more base parts of the male gaze.

Amanda, do not get discouraged. Rather, let that night be a lesson for you. The discomfort that you experienced was evidence that you do already possess an innate sense of Christian modesty, and that is why you felt like you wanted to leave and go home. Remember the lesson that you learned: it is modesty that safeguards chastity.

Chastity is a beautiful, comely, attractive virtue, that inspires instinctive horror of all that could tarnish it. When it is encountered, it inspires awe and reverence. This is wonderfully expressed in the Book of Wisdom: *O how beautiful is the chaste generation with glory: for the memory thereof is immortal: because it is known both with God and with men.*[20] Why is chastity so glorious and beautiful? Precisely because it makes manifest the strength of soul of the one who possesses it, and the dignity of the body that it honours, whereas unchastity reveals a weak soul, one that is slave to its lusts and treats the body as if it were hardly more than that of an animal.

Some people think that by engaging in unchaste actions, they are making a show of power and strength. In reality, consenting to lustful thoughts or actions reveals a weak soul, one that is unable to control itself, that is enslaved to base passions. Often, it is true, such souls do not realise their state of slavery until they have the grace to get out of the mire. And then they are appalled by how weak they were. God, through His infinite mercy and love for human beings, in spite of our transgressions and weaknesses, allows even for souls who may have been chained for years in unchaste behaviour—if they truly seek after it and are faithful to the graces He sends—to recover chastity and even, to a certain extent, virginity. One only needs to look at the many saints who had this experience—St Augustine, St Mary of Egypt and St Margaret of Cortona to name only a few of the most famous. After these saints cast off the chains of unchastity, they rose to dizzying heights of true love of God and neighbour. At the same time, their past actions served as a constant reminder of the fragility of their human nature and their constant need of grace.

So remember, Amanda, chastity is a virtue of strength! Its acquisition and deepening requires time and effort. Until we get there, and even when we do, we must be aware of how fragile the virtue of chastity is and foster very carefully the virtue of modesty which guards it.

Modesty as Virtue and Fruit

There are some beautiful distinctions in Catholic teaching that can enlighten our understanding of modesty. Many people think that when referring to modesty we speak only of clothing, whereas true modesty encompasses and is reflected in every part of an individual's behaviour, both internal and external. Clothing, of itself, makes one neither modest nor chaste. This is why, strictly speaking, the fact that a woman is fully clothed does not mean that she is necessarily modest or chaste. It might only be because in her culture she is required to dress that way, or because her husband does not want other men admiring her. It is well known that sexual abuse and infidelity exist also in cultures and groups (such as Islam or the Amish) where female attire is objectively impeccable. On the other hand, there are women—like some of the friends you mentioned— who think that modesty is essentially an internal attitude that does not necessarily determine how one actually dresses. Both these attitudes are off the mark, for while it is true that one can be modestly dressed without having the virtue of modesty, it is not possible to have that virtue if one dresses immodestly, for as I explained in my earlier letter, the body influences the soul and makes manifest its intentions. It is essential to understand that for the Christian, modesty is a natural virtue which can be elevated by grace to the supernatural realm and lead to the heights of sanctity. As one practices this virtue, one becomes more virtuous, and sanctifying grace increases in the soul. So, we can already see here that it is not just a matter of having modesty or not, but rather of growing in modesty, of becoming more modest.

In addition to the virtues, the soul in the state of grace also has the Seven Gifts of the Holy Spirit, which allow us to be more docile in following prompts or inspirations we may have in trying to grow in supernatural virtue. Unlike the virtues that we can practice ourselves at any moment, the Gifts allow us to be moved directly by the Holy Spirit when He chooses. If we compare the virtues to a row boat in which the effort to move forward is provided by the rower, the Gifts are more like sails that the Holy Spirit can move at any time, pushing us forward to our destination much quicker, much more effectively, with greater ease and less effort. Therefore, the more an individual is faithful to the promptings and inspirations of the Holy Spirit, the more the Gifts of the Holy Spirit are manifest in them, and a more rapid growth in virtue occurs.

As the Gifts lead to more good actions because the soul is more docile to grace, they ultimately produce what we call the Fruits of the Holy Spirit. These Fruits are in effect the sign of consistent fidelity to the Holy Spirit's inspirations. And this is where we meet once again the idea of modesty, now as one of the mature fruits of living in harmony with divine grace. *The fruit of the Spirit is, charity, joy, peace, patience, benignity, goodness, longanimity, mildness, faith, modesty, continency, chastity.*[21] What this means is that, the more we progress in love of God and attentiveness to His grace in our souls, the more the Holy Spirit in Person moves us to perform even greater acts of virtue that will eventually produce some delicious fruit that will be a joy for God and for the world.

In your own case, as demonstrated by your initial letter, it is evident that the natural virtue of modesty was instilled in you by your mother during your childhood. This natural modesty then made it somewhat easier for you to be docile to the inspiration of the Holy Spirit in pursuing the supernatural virtue of modesty, made manifest, for example, in your deciding to wear the veil for God alone. Docility to the Holy Spirit's inspirations has allowed you to realise that what matters the most is not the world's customs, but God's commandments. If you continue to follow these inspirations, the Gifts will become more and more operative in you and will soon produce fruit; then you will truly take delight in being modest; it will become second nature to you because it is the Holy Spirit in person who will be driving this spiritual growth.

True modesty then is the sign that a woman is conscious of God Himself dwelling in her heart; it is the result of both natural and supernatural virtue and docility to the inspirations of the Holy Spirit. It makes her a profound edification for all those who see her. Modesty in dress and behaviour is, therefore, an indispensable way of making us more attentive to the obligations which we contracted at our Baptism. "Modesty protects the intimate centre of the person. It means refusing to unveil what should remain hidden. It is ordered to chastity to whose sensitivity it bears witness. It guides how one looks at others and behaves toward them in conformity with the dignity of persons".[22]

Modesty and the Mutual Attraction of the Sexes

Amanda, having just described to you the true definition of Christian Modesty and how it plays a key role in the safeguarding of the virtue of chastity, I must mention something about the key differences in how males and females can fall prey to sins against chastity. First, let's consider how things happen in the sub-human world. In animals, the reproductive instinct is mainly moderated by seasons; the urge to reproduce is purely biological. When the female is fertile, she adopts an attitude that attracts the male and excretes hormones that entice the male to copulation. Neither of the animals "know" what they are doing, nor why they are doing it. God gave them an instinct so that each species would last upon the earth, but none of them has ever been able to perceive the link between copulation and the birthing that takes place a certain number of weeks or months later, depending on the species. With humans, things are very different. While it is true that fertile women also put out pheromones that attract males, it is usually the *sight* of the potential mate that arouses the sexual instinct. When adolescents reach puberty, their sexual organs become capable of generating or conceiving, and nature gives them an inclination to unite with the other sex. But unlike animals, it does not take young humans long to suspect that making love is somehow linked with making babies, even though the exact way in which this happens is made known to them only gradually. It does not require much reflection to understand that if one engages in intercourse, one must be prepared to welcome the child who may be born from the union. This preparation involves a commitment of the man and woman to each other, for the reason that the education of a child is a work that demands much energy and concerted effort for many years. To willingly bring a child into the world without the support of a mother and father is irresponsible. In other words, it is only in marriage that such activity should take place. Until married, one must be careful not to find oneself in a position that could compromise the virtue of chastity, and open oneself to possibly becoming a parent without really being in a position to be one.

All that you are already aware of, Amanda. What you probably are not aware of—very few women are, to tell the truth—is that the attraction to the opposite sex has different manifestations in males and in females. Women long to be loved, to be held, to be protected; they also have an instinctive desire for children. I'm sure when you were younger— and perhaps still today!—you would sometimes dream of your Prince Charming coming to protect and save you, and you would hug and embrace and live happily ever after. Well, things are different for the male. Whereas women are more attracted to romantic, emotional intimacy and, as they mature, long for a baby, men are more attracted to women, and that attraction, far from remaining at the level of the romantic Prince Charming model, tends, even at a young age, to be quite anatomical. From an early age males get very curious about the workings of human intimacy, and that means they are curious about the details of the female body.

You may find this a bit confronting, but it is important that you be aware of it. It actually makes sense, because it is the male who is the active principle in human procreation. He must explore and find a way *into* a woman's intimacy. He must find a mate, and when he has found her, he must "know" her, to use the biblical expression. Genesis says that Adam "knew" Eve, not that Eve "knew" Adam. She will, of course, but only because Adam knew her first, that is to say, he found a way into her intimacy, and entrusted to her the most intimate part of himself, that is to say, the seed of a potential human being. That is what the Bible means by saying that a man "knows" his wife. No one else can know her that way. Only her husband has that right and privilege.

This very simple truth suffices to explain why it is that men have in themselves an innate desire to get to know females better, even in the details, and the first step towards that is to *see them*. It also explains the innate desire young women have to *be seen by* males, to let themselves be found, chased, won over by them (though again, there is a big difference in the way men and women understand what is involved in the seeing). Such an innate desire must be trained so that the woman allows herself to be won, not by just any man, but by the one she loves, the one she wants to spend her life with, the one she wants to be the father of her children, him and no other. All this is of universal experience. In the tender years of childhood and adolescence, parents must protect the intimacy of their daughters, and they must train their sons to honour the female sex as one to be loved and respected, not used and violated (even in thought). This is essential so that the intimate "knowledge" of the spouse be safeguarded for marriage. Another way of expressing all this is to say that woman's attraction to man is more psychological, whereas man's attraction to woman is more physical. Hence, man is much more easily tempted by scanty feminine attire than vice versa.

These differences are precisely the reason for which sins against the Sixth and Ninth Commandments have different origins and manifestations in males and females. Whereas females are often led to such sins by their emotions and imagination, desiring to be held and loved,—whence the morally dangerous feminine consumption of romantic novels or movies—, men are far more likely to fall into such sins by seeing the female body — whence the proliferation of pornography which is one of the most grievous forms of sexual abuse and slavery that has ever afflicted the human race, for it enslaves at once its producers, its actors and its consumers. This is precisely why the sight of a scantily dressed woman is often the trigger of such sins in men, while it is not necessarily so in women.

Men know this and priests often hear of their struggles. My spiritual sons frequently speak to me of their battles for purity, which are made exponentially more difficult due to the display of female flesh and form that is available in every city and on virtually every television channel, internet page, and even tragically within many Catholic churches, including traditional ones. Amanda, I want to stress that I am not speaking of female *intentionality*. I would go as far as to say that the vast majority of women have no ill intentions whatsoever when dressing (including the scantily dressed ones); they simply do not know better or do not fully realise the effect their dress has on men, or so I hope. However, regardless of their intentions, the effect remains. And it is this that I am trying to stress as a spiritual father of both daughters and sons. I want to shield my spiritual sons from constant and grave temptation and falls, and I want to protect my spiritual daughters from being the unintentional cause of such storms of temptation and falls into mortal sin.

This natural desire that men have to see women has been deeply wounded by sin. Fallen nature in man tells him: "any woman I see I can have". Reason interjects: "yes, but there is only one you are *allowed* to have, and that's your wife". But if the way a woman is clothed reveals to him her flesh and the intimate shape of her body, the unspoken message his reason gets from the woman, even if it would never occur to her, is: "this is my body, I'm happy for you to know it in its details; enjoy if you will, I don't mind". And when the dominant culture tells him that he can have any woman that will allow him, then his reason is obscured and he has no argument to persuade the will. Unless something comes to distract his attention, the fall into mortal sin can be swift. Healing can only come through repentance and conversion to practicing the faith, for without it men do not have the grace to be chaste.

This is not to downplay the role of a man in fostering virtue, practicing custody of the eyes and battling concupiscence. Indeed, it is imperative that he must do this also. Men cannot blame women for their sins of impurity, nor do they get a free pass when it comes to modesty! But, in the context of this letter, Amanda, I am focusing primarily on the role that a female can play for her own edification and that of her neighbour.

Amanda, if man has a natural desire to uncover your intimacy, you want him to have to take a lot of time and effort to do so, because first you must be certain of his love, his honour, his virtue, his will to stand by you (and the child who may come of your union) no matter what. You first want him to get to know *you*, you as a person, your gifts and talents. Only at the very end of a long acquaintance, once you are certain of his virtue, will you allow him to enter into the intimacy of your body. That is the very last step that takes place *after* marriage, not before. You need to carefully preserve the secret intimacy of your being, and one day you will commit it to your husband in a lifelong, fecund bond. Unless the Lord calls you to the religious life or consecrated virginity, in which case that secret intimacy will be for no man but for Christ alone, who will make you spiritually fecund in a truly nuptial bond with Himself.

Modesty as a Check for Curiosity and Custody of the Senses

Amanda, I speak openly to you here as to a spiritual daughter. I do so as the father of your soul, for which I will have to give an account. Woman is the most beautiful part of God's creation. When God created the universe,

He saved the best for last, creating Eve after Adam. She is the most beautiful of all. God made her so beautiful, in order that man would be drawn to her and that the human race would be propagated on the earth. It is nothing to be afraid of, but it is something you must be aware of. Do keep in mind this: the beauty you have from God is *amplified* through the eyes of a man, and it is your modesty that helps keep his curiosity in check.

Let's recall a story. King David was not just a good man; he was a prophet, favoured by God in so many ways, a great saint. On this particular day, he stayed at home in idleness while his army went out to battle. *It happened that David arose from his bed after noon, and walked upon the roof of the king's house: and he saw from the roof of his house a woman washing herself, over against him: and the woman was very beautiful.*[23] The beauty of the woman attracts him, he is allured, and consents to adultery in his heart, according to those words of Our Lord: *Whosoever shall look on a woman to lust after her, hath already committed adultery with her in his heart.*[24] From there to the act of adultery and the subsequent murder of her husband, there was only one step. But it all began with his eyes seeing a lovely woman bathing. A holy man sees a woman bathing and he falls into adultery and murder. That's food for thought. This Biblical story makes manifest the importance of modest dress. Certain forms of dress appeal directly to the senses. They seem designed not to clothe the body, but to reveal as much of it as possible. The eye quickly perceives this, and passions are promptly aroused.

Lack of custody of the senses leads to unhealthy and unholy curiosity. This is what lost David (by the way, have you ever wondered what Bathsheba was doing bathing in sight of the king's balcony? Would you bathe where you could be seen by anyone unless you had bad intentions?). Curiosity is the cause of so many sins—it is, after all, what lost Eve who, even in her preternatural state, was curious to have the knowledge of Good and Evil. Just look at how advertisements work. Have you noticed how, often in order to sell anything—a car, a house, a swimming pool...—, a scantily clad woman will appear on the scene? Advertisers know that by putting the woman there, most men will have a close look at the advertisement in order to see the woman, and they will be more inclined to purchase.

In day to day life, if there is an opening to male curiosity—because your skirt is short, or the neckline plunges low or the whole thing fits so tightly that the shape of your body is all too evident—then you can be absolutely certain that most of the men who see you will be curious to see more. That is the law of fallen human nature. To be ignorant of it is tragic; to ignore it willingly is sinful folly.

I believe I can hear you thinking : "but if the men were chaste, I wouldn't have to worry about my clothing!" To a certain extent that is true, but it is equally true that you need to help the men be chaste by having reverence for your own body. If you don't revere your own body by covering it modestly, why would the men? Do not ever entertain such thoughts as "how dirty-minded these men are". Some are, some are not, but they are all men, all part of a fallen race. One of the most arduous efforts men have to make in this life when they want to be virtuous is to keep that natural inclination in check. If you have respect for a man, you will want to help him. In the case of really virtuous men, I can assure you that when they see women dressed in such a revealing way, it causes them grief. First of all for her soul, which is certainly in danger, but also because such a man has much more to offer her than what she seems to be appealing to in him by means of the exhibition of her flesh and/ or form. Traditional forms of dress give the serenity to see and to get to know someone without the distraction of the flesh. But when that screen is not there, the offer appeals to the most base passions in man. In conclusion, if a man ever suggests that a woman should wear more modest clothing, never think for a moment that he must have a dirty mind.

It's actually quite the opposite! If he had a dirty mind, he would be quite happy to gaze at what she so imprudently shows him of her body, and he will want to see even more. No, Amanda, the men that promote modesty in dress are not dirty-minded. They want you to help them, and they really want to help you do so.

You see, you mustn't be like Cain who, when God asked where his brother Abel was, answered: *Am I my brother's keeper?*[25] The answer was, well yes, to a certain extent we are all our brothers' and sisters' keepers. We need to help each other. *Love thy neighbour as thyself.*[26] A godly woman who is aware of this will take care not to unintentionally be the occasion of the fall of an otherwise good man. There are many stories of men, both young and old, who have fallen into mortal sin—and sometimes many mortal sins—because they saw a beautiful woman dressed in a way reminiscent of Eve clad with her fig leaves. Their natural curiosity about the opposite sex led them to stare, and this aroused in them a passion they could not resist. *Gaze not upon a maiden; lest her beauty be a stumbling block to thee.... For many have perished by the beauty of a woman, and thereby lust is enkindled as a fire.*[27]

Modesty in Words

Something must be added here about modesty and chastity in words, because often it is immodesty in words that leads to immodesty in deeds. Words refer to ideas, to things. These things in turn evoke images and desires. If I explain to someone in detail the delicious meal I had yesterday, it may very well evoke in them a desire to have the same; it may make them hungry, and begin to salivate. So it is with the procreative instinct. If we speak of these things, the words can easily arouse a desire to experience what is spoken of. Now, regarding nutrition, we must eat to survive, and so, to speak of food is perfectly legitimate. The act of procreation, however, is not necessary for individual existence, but for the longevity of the race. This longevity is dependent not only on the act of procreation, but also on its manner and time. It matters little if you eat this or that at this time or that time, but carnal union is possible with only one person, and that in specific circumstances that preserve its intimacy. Therefore, one must take great care not to arouse that instinct in others, unless in the proper context with one's spouse. The practical consequences of this are that one should not speak of the sexual organs, nor should one refer to persons or events or actions that would lead naturally to thinking about them. This is also why St Paul warns the Ephesians: *Fornication, and all uncleanness, or covetousness, let it not so much as be named among you, as becometh saints*.[28]

Chastity in words includes choosing the right words when one has to refer to such things. It is indicative of an overly sexualised society that one not infrequently hears reference to these things using words that in former times would have remained veiled. For example, people often refer to "having sex", but this expression, by its explicit reference to copulation which is common to all animals, does not leave any space for the proper protection of intimacy. Our elders would have used other expressions such as the "marital embrace" or "conjugal relations", much like God Himself does by using the verb "to know" when referring to Adam and Eve's first union as man and wife. In the same way, it is sadly rather common to hear reference to the organs of reproduction using their anatomical names, whereas chaste persons tend to prefer such expressions as "private parts". It is one of the tactics of the enemy to get people accustomed to sinning by breaking down the social barriers to mentioning sinful actions. In a word, when people have the word "sex" frequently on their lips, they have it frequently on their minds, which increases temptations and leads to thinking that sinning is normal.

This is why St Francis de Sales was able to write: "Purity has its source in the heart, but it is in the body that its material results take shape, and therefore it may be forfeited both by the exterior senses and by the thoughts and desires of the heart. All lack of modesty in seeing, hearing, speaking, smelling or touching, is impurity, especially when the heart takes pleasure therein".[29]

So my advice to you, my daughter, is to be modest and chaste in your words. Do not refer to anything that concerns your intimacy in any way, except of course when you need to share something with your mother, your doctor, or with the priest in the confessional. Friends might deride you for not taking part in lewd conversations, but don't pay any attention to them. Guard your interior castle, that is to say your Christian soul, and its temple, that is your body, with great care, and you will find much peace.

Modesty in Behaviour

Amanda, I understand and have also heard from numerous women that they simply have no understanding of how their dress and behaviours affect men. There are certain positions and actions that are tolerable in a man, but which a lady must avoid in public. For example, while it is perfectly permissible when on your own or with your sister to lie down on the floor, you should not do this when there are others, especially men, around. Nor does a lady stretch her arms or spread out her legs in the presence of a man. Wearing a modest dress, almost automatically and of its own, will give you the instinct to avoid these things, but when you are wearing trousers or even shorts, it is not so. In the same way you should not adjust your undergarments in the presence of others or touch the intimate parts of your body. These are things that everyone used to learn, but here and there one now notices a lack of education in these matters, even in adults. Nor is it appropriate for women in churches or any public place to bow themselves down to the ground in adoration, for anyone coming from behind would have their backside in full view!

In former times, custom and education were enough for them to know this instinctively, but now they need to listen to the men who have the courage and the charity to tell them. By her modesty a woman can use her charm to tame the passions of man; by her immodesty her beauty becomes a stumbling block to man. Like it or not, this makes women the guardians of chastity in the world. This is why God has given woman a much more delicate sense of modesty than man, not only to protect her own integrity, but also to protect man against the fury of his own passions. When woman is modest, man has only himself to blame if he succumbs to temptations of the flesh. But when woman decides to display parts of her body which should be covered, she is no longer a helper, but can easily become—in spite of her intentions—a seductress, sharing in the guilt of man.

The Sin of Immodesty

As for whether or not the way you dressed that night was a mortal sin, let me first say a few words about what mortal sin is. To commit a mortal sin is to lose God's grace, to fall into a state of enmity with God; it is to be dead spiritually. To die in that state is to be condemned to eternal hellfire, for there is no conversion possible after death. St Paul's words are clear: *Know you not, that you are the temple of God, and that the Spirit of God dwelleth in you? But if any man violate the temple of God, him shall God destroy. For the temple of God is holy, which you are.*[30] I therefore commend you on not wanting to commit a mortal sin.

However, even though it is good that you do not want to commit a mortal sin, it would be better if you wanted to avoid sin altogether. To ask the question as to where the borderline is from venial to mortal sin manifests little love for Our Lord. There are plenty of people who want to avoid mortal sin because they don't want to go to Hell. I would like for my spiritual daughter to want to avoid all sin because it hurts Our Lord. God wants excellence. He does not want you to drift along with the crowd, or to compare yourself with the worst and say you are OK. No, He wants you to excel in chastity and modesty. This requires intentionality on your part. I want you to be chaste, not just to avoid sins of impurity. Many Catholics, sadly, do not have the love of chastity. Their mentality is often: if it weren't sinful and going to lead to Hell, I would do it. That clearly is not love for chastity. It is a slave's fear of Hell.

Coming to a direct answer to the question you asked, your outfit that day was objectively speaking gravely contrary to the moral law. The reason for this is that a man who has not mastered his passions—and most have not—will have immediately seen you as an object for pleasure and would have indulged in gazing at you, committing impurity in his heart (cf. Mt 5:28)—as you noticed they did—, whereas a virtuous man will have had to turn away in order not to look at you that way. You fell into the exact scenario Pope Pius XII evoked when he said: "How many young girls there are who do not see any wrongdoing in following certain shameless styles like so many sheep. They certainly would blush if they could guess the impression they make and the feelings they evoke in those who see them".[31] If you had been fully aware of this and conscious that your immodesty could cause mortal sin in men who would see you, you would certainly have committed a mortal sin by wearing it, even if you were hoping that would not happen. What this teaches you is that sometimes apparently "innocent" actions can have grave consequences, for mortal sin can be committed in thought alone.

Sometimes you hear people say that it's just a matter of not looking at someone with lust, as if one could hit a switch and all would be fixed. Such nonsense ignores the reality of concupiscence that flows from Original Sin and that is present in *every* man you will ever meet. In all my study of theology I have yet to find reference to any but *one* Immaculate Conception... It is true that there is a very small percentage of very virtuous men who have trained themselves for a very long time in self-mastery, who could possibly have been able to look at you that night and speak to you with tranquility, but only because of a great mastery over themselves, and even then there is a risk (remember David). It is a torture you should not put them through. Sometimes good men find themselves in gatherings (even in churches, sad to say) where they have nowhere to look except the floor if they do not want to feel the bite of lust, so widespread is immodesty in dress. In the circumstances, however, as you explained them to me, your clothing that day was due more to youthful folly than anything else. Explain this when you go to confession. And in the future remember your personal dignity, and help the men that see you do the same.

Amanda, everything God asks us to do has its challenges. Being a Catholic has never been easy. So if what I have written here causes a visceral reaction in you, maybe sit down and ask yourself why that is, pray with it, struggle with it, grow with it. You will not regret it.

Also, never forget the sting of conscience you felt that night. Do not ignore your conscience or try to numb it, for conscience is the very voice of God to keep you on the straight and narrow path that leads to eternal life. *Enter ye in at the narrow gate: for wide is the gate, and broad is the way that leadeth to destruction, and many there are who go in thereat. How narrow is the gate, and strait is the way that leadeth to life: and few there are that find it!*[32]

A couple of final points. When you realise you are off track, don't make it worse by drinking! That was a very foolish thing to do, and it could have ended in disaster. More than one young woman in that same situation has lost her virginity and even found herself pregnant.

Also, never stay away from praying or from church

because you think you have failed, or even if you have fallen into some serious sin. It is then that you need it the most! Any thought of shortening prayer or not going to church is infallibly from the devil. Besides, it is precisely your life of prayer that has given you the instinct of modesty that tormented you on that night. So whenever you have any thought of seeking consolation in creatures and omitting or shortening your prayers, do not listen, but rather do the opposite. Pray more!

With my blessing,

Your Father in Christ

THIRD CORRESPONDENCE

Modesty in the Context of
Modern Culture

Be Not Conformed to This World

Rm 12:2

2 July 2023
Feast of the Visitation of Our Lady

Dear Father,

I cannot thank you enough for the time you have taken to provide such clear answers to my questions. I am especially grateful for the detail you went into explaining Original Sin and concupiscence and how it is always going to rear its ugly head. It gave me so much to think about.

However, I hope you do not mind, Father, but I had some more specific questions that I could perhaps address to others, but I thought it best to ask you, given you have been helping me understand this so much in detail.

Father, one of the arguments I always hear when modesty comes up is how important it is to view modesty in its cultural context. I think what people mean by that is that modesty can actually take on different forms in different cultures. If this is true, does this mean that it is OK to wear certain things because it is widespread today?

I already sort of know the answer to this question, because of my last letter to you. Even though most of the girls were dressed immodestly, I still guessed instinctively it wasn't right. Furthermore, if that culture thing is true, then it must be fine to wear a bikini to the beach as so many women do, but I wouldn't be seen dead in one of those! And I know there are even nudist beaches where people have no clothing at all (as shocking as that sounds!); so if the culture context theory is right, it would be OK to be naked on those beaches!? But that can't be right. I think I sense the answer, but I just can't find the right words to make a good response to the cultural objection I frequently hear, even from very good and modest people.

And I guess what I am specifically wondering after your last letter, is where do I draw the line if I want to be serious about my faith and not offend Our Lord? I understand fully that the dress I wore to that birthday party I wrote to you about was immodest. I will never dress like that again, I promise! (I actually made a big bonfire the other day and burnt it along with several others items from my wardrobe that I now know are immodest...).

But does this mean I always have to dress like Our Lady...? Isn't that being prudish? And am I not allowed to follow the fashions like the other girls? Or do I always have to wear dresses that are shapeless, and cover the ankles and wrists?

And is it sinful to wear makeup or style my hair or wear high heels? And if it is, how will I ever find a husband? And when I do get married, am I not supposed to dress in a way that pleases my husband? But what if he wants me to wear short dresses or low neck-lines or transparent fabrics?

With gratitude for your time, through Christ,

Amanda

Beyond fashion and its demands, there are higher and
more pressing laws, principles superior to fashion,
and unchangeable, which under no circumstances
can be sacrificed to the whim of pleasure or fancy,
and before which must bow the fleeting omnipotence
of fashion.
These principles have been proclaimed
by God, by the Church, by the Saints, by reason,
by Christian morality.

Venerable Pope Pius XII

15 August 2023
Feast of the Assumption of Our Lady

Dear Amanda,

Your simple and direct questions reflect much of the confusion that abounds in today's society. I will again try and answer in the way that I think may be of some help.

Fashions in History

First of all, let's go back to that definition of modesty I gave last time. Modesty fixes the mode, the manner in which decency is protected. This of itself implies that there is a different measure for different people and different periods in history. But all these differences, when we look at everything we know from antiquity up until the middle of the last century, amounted to very little. If you compare a Roman matriarch of the first century with an English peasant of the tenth and a French queen of the fourteenth, you will notice a number of variants in the way dresses are made, but you will essentially observe the same care to hide the flesh and areas of the shape that inflame the male passions (the breasts and the posterior). The modes of dress always maintained feminine features such as the type of cloth used, the shape of the skirt and the details on the waist. After the French Revolution transparent fabrics become more common, and the cuts of the dresses start to expose and highlight bare flesh much more, especially that of the décolletage. Even though this last feature can be found in other periods as well, it has always been frowned upon by the Church.

All of humanity, in every culture, has always been careful about the essentials, and has been particularly attentive to this when it comes to female attire, for reasons that I expounded in the previous letter. It is so true that G.K.

Chesterton writes: "Have you ever noticed how true is that old phrase, *clothed and in his right mind* (Mk 5:15)? Man is not in his right mind when he is not clothed with the symbols of his social dignity. Humanity is not even human when it is naked".[33] This is why Pope Pius XII, in a long address on fashions, summarised the teaching in this way: "There always exists an absolute norm to be preserved, no matter how broad and changeable the relative morals of styles may be ... Style may never give a proximate occasion of sin, and clothing must be a shield against disordered sensuality".[34]

It is clear that Christianity, with its teaching on the dignity of the human person redeemed by Christ, has something to add, in that clothing also becomes an essential element of protection for the adopted sons and daughters of God, helping them to preserve the state of grace to which God has so graciously called them. Furthermore, Catholics are missionaries at heart and should want to convert the whole world to Christ, and not be converted to the world and its ways. This was made evident from the apostolic era in which the apostles constantly called the faithful to be on their guard against sexual immorality and promiscuity, and called them to distance themselves from the ways of the world and be conformed to Christ.[35] Up until very recently, the Church for the most part followed that command and remained distant from the ways of the world. In the past decades however, especially since the Second Vatican Council, a growing tendency to be seen as "in touch with the world" has caused many to drop their guard and to begin to dress (and undress...) like everyone else.

Fashions That Offend God

I mentioned above that the norm of modesty throughout history has varied little. There was only one category of women who could be seen to depart from this norm; that category was women who sell their bodies for pleasure. It is a sad fact—it is indeed an indisputable one for anyone who takes a serene look at history—that many of the fashions we see today, in former times were the unmistakable mark of women of ill-repute. This is not to say that all the women who adopt these fashions today have bad intentions. I am just stressing the reality: at the very least, it sends a signal that esteem for chastity has been lost. And this is truly heartbreaking to see.

Already in 1941, Pope Pius XII lamented: "...Many believing and even pious women... by accepting to follow such or such bold fashion, cause to disappear by their example the last hesitations which keep the crowd of their sisters far from this fashion which may become for them a cause of spiritual ruin. As long as certain alluring attires remain the sad privilege of women of doubtful reputation and, as it were, the sign at which they may be recognised, no one will dare to adopt them for oneself. But the day these attires appear to be worn by persons who are above all suspicion, there will no longer be any hesitation to follow the tide, a tide which may cause the worst falls".[36]

Today, we need more and more laity to stand up and reset by their good example the standard where it should be, holding high the banner of Christian modesty, regardless of any criticism they might receive. Amanda, you will be chastised by some, especially in prestigious and fashionable circles, if you persevere in dressing as a modest woman should. You will be accused of being old-fashioned, of wanting to go back to the Middle Ages, of wanting to impose on every woman to don a Mother Hubbard Dress,[37] of not being in touch with your times, and many worse insinuations will come your way. Stand firm, you know the truth. Remain faithful to your God, and your God will reward you with an ineffable peace that those who seek to please the world can never even imagine.

Remember, too, that we were forewarned about this. Our Lady told St Jacinta Marto in 1919: "Certain fashions are to be introduced which will offend Our Lord very much. Those who serve God should not follow these fashions. The Church has no fashions". St Jacinta also confirmed what we already knew (in particular through St Alphonsus Liguori): "The sins which hurl most souls into Hell, are the sins of the flesh".

Three centuries earlier, Our Lady had appeared to Venerable Mother Mariana de Jesus Torres in Quito, Ecuador in the 17th century with a message of warning for the end of the 19th century and especially the 20th century. The following words are taken from this Church approved apparition, known as Our Lady of Good Success: "...in these unhappy times, there will be unbridled lust which, acting thus to snare the rest into sin, will conquer innumerable frivolous souls who will be lost. Innocence will almost no longer be found in children, nor modesty in women, and in this supreme moment of need of the Church, those who should speak will fall silent".

Amanda, I want you to be clear about this: whether we like it or not, women are the moral compass of society. If they are aware of this and dress modestly, the level of morality rises. If they are not, the level of morality descends. Today it is reaching an all-time low, which in all honesty gives reason to fear a complete breakdown of morality. It is no secret that the world is increasingly ensnared and enslaved by lust.

It can also be helpful to look at the way saints reacted to immodest dress. Fr. Stefano M. Manelli writes: "A strict insistence on this particular point is a constant in the lives of all the Saints, from the Apostle, St. Paul (telling the woman to wear a veil so that she may not need to have her head appear 'as if she were shorn': [1 Cor 11:5-6]), to St John Chrysostom, St Ambrose, etc., down to Padre Pio of Pietrelcina, who would permit no halfway measures, but always insisted on modest dresses clearly below the knees".[38]

In fact, concerning the latter, if their dresses were low-cut or too short when coming to confession, St Pio would refuse them the sacrament and send them away. As dresses in the 1960's became scantier and scantier, he sent larger and larger numbers of women away. It got to a point where his fellow friars posted a sign on the door of the church which read: "By Padre Pio's explicit wish, women must enter the confessional wearing skirts at least 8 inches below the knee. It is forbidden to borrow longer dresses in church and to wear them to confession". Why 8 inches *below* the knee? Simply because the miniskirt recently introduced was brazenly announcing 8 inches *above* the knee... If those whom he refused asked why he treated them in this manner, St Pio would answer: "Don't you know what pain it costs me to shut the door on anyone? The Lord has forced me to do so. I do not call anyone, nor do I refuse anyone either. There is someone else who calls and refuses them. I am His useless tool".[39] Indeed, would it have been right to grant these women absolution while dressed in an indecent manner? To absolve from sins a woman who, just before entering and just after leaving the confessional, could be the cause of sins in others? Which brings back again the question of immodest dresses at weddings. Is it right for a woman to stand before God's altar with her maids of honour to receive the sacrament of matrimony while at the very same time being an occasion of sin by her immodest dress?

On this hear St. John Chrysostom, one of the most illustrious Fathers of the Church: "When you have made another sin in his heart, how can you be innocent? Tell me, whom does this world condemn? Whom do judges in court punish? Those who drink poison or those who prepare it and administer the fatal potion? You have prepared the abominable cup, you have given the death-dealing drink, and you are more criminal than are those who poison the body; you murder not the body, but the soul. And it is not to enemies you do this, nor are you urged on by any imaginary necessity, nor provoked by injury, but out of foolish vanity and pride".

An Out of Place Objection

Sometimes you will run into people who contend that in former times an immodestly dressed woman was an occasion of sin for men because it was a rare sight (such as the prostitute mentioned above). But nowadays, if virtually all women are dressed immodestly, men will be so accustomed to it that it is no longer an occasion of sin: *ab assuetis non fit passio – the passions are not aroused by things we are accustomed to.* How are we to answer this objection?

Pope Pius XII called this objection both insidious and out of place.[40] While it is true that customary sights may not always arouse an immediate temptation, they do register in one's consciousness. A man walking down the street who encounters ten women in miniskirts will not be tempted to stop and stare at each one, perhaps not at any. But he has seen them and they remain in his memory. The picture of them may fade from the mind, but suddenly, that evening, or days or even years later, it will emerge from the attic of the mind and may bring on a violent attack against holy purity. Concupiscence often lies dormant, but it *never* dies in a normal man. Nine successive looks at a half-dressed woman may fail to arouse concupiscence of the flesh, but the tenth may prove fatal to the soul. Never forget that, Amanda; and it does not matter how old or how holy a man is. Nor does it matter how holy she might be. Tertullian has a word of caution for such women: "A holy woman may be beautiful by the gift of nature, but she must not give occasion to lust. If beauty be hers, so far from setting it off, she ought rather to obscure it." By those words, he did not mean to say disfigure it, but conceal it by modest clothing and veiling.

I have already mentioned the example of King David. Another case in point is that of St Benedict. St Gregory tells us that when he was living alone as a hermit in a very austere way—praying, fasting, dwelling in a cave—, one day his imagination (no doubt at the instigation of the devil) brought back to his mind a woman he had seen in his father's house and who was quite a bit older than him. The temptation of impurity became so fierce that the young Benedict was on the verge of giving in and going back to Rome to find that woman. It was then that by divine inspiration he removed his clothes and threw himself into a patch of briars, rolling over and over in them until his entire body was covered with bleeding wounds. The fire of pain put out the fire of lust in his flesh.

Why am I telling you this story? Because, it was the *sight of a woman he had seen years before* that caused such a violent rush of passion that nearly destroyed the young Benedict. Imagine how things would be today if he had succumbed to that temptation. We would never have had the father of western monasticism; there would have been no Benedictine order, no Benedictine saints, no monasteries of monks or nuns, no patron saint of Europe. If anyone tells you that men get used to seeing half-naked women, smile at their nonsense, but set their mind straight on this point: they are in fairy land, in denial of reality. That reality is the volatile frailty of human nature caused by Original Sin and its proneness to evil.

True Beauty

Amanda, you will no doubt encounter people who will tell you that you are being prudish. The word comes from the French "prudefemme" which means an excellent woman, one who is wise and prudent in her words and actions. It is therefore virtually synonymous with modesty, and modesty is not prudery in the modern sense, but prudence in the sense that true wisdom presides over the choice of clothing. The meaning of the word has evolved, of course, as words do. Today prudishness or prudery is used as a scarecrow for modest women, turning them to ridicule. A "prudish" woman nowadays is one who wants every woman to wear a formless dress going all the way down to the ankles and wrists and with a collar up to the chin. Sadly, many Catholic women have a morbid fear of ridicule, and yet ridicule is often the last resort of persons who have no real arguments. When you are faced with that, Amanda, you need to stand your ground and, if you sense there is a real desire for dialogue, initiate them to the true meaning of Christian modesty, which is not prudery, but an instinct that is both natural and supernatural, one that can save us from ourselves and our disordered passions.

Modest attire also has the priceless benefit of giving women the strength to present themselves as persons, not as objects, and therefore protects them from exploitation. Did you know that at most university health centres, the top two prescribed drugs are anti-depressants and contraceptives?[41] It seems clear that the sexual promiscuity of our day does not lead to freedom but to enslavement, and consequently, to depression. You do not want to go that path. A woman wants to be loved as a person, not lusted after like a piece of meat. If she is treated like the latter, it can only pull her down psychologically. And if she exhibits her body by dressing immodestly, she is setting herself up for precisely that. Modesty has the singular advantage of stressing your natural beauty without the disadvantage of making you an object of lust.

You ask how you will ever find a husband if you dress modestly. I have partially answered that in my previous letter, in which I made it clear that what attracts a man to you must be primarily your person, not your body. If you are to be married, you must one day find a good man. By good man, I of course mean one who is virtuous and hard-working, one who will be faithful to you and be a good, strong father to your children. His looks matter little. And the same goes for you. If you really love those children to whom you may one day give birth and if you love the man who is their father, then you want him to find in you all that makes for a truly virtuous and hard-working wife and mother.

You can see right away that the way you appeal to him should not be primarily through your physical beauty. God has gifted you at that level. Furthermore, your beauty is such that you need to do little for it to appear. You should therefore not go out of your way to do so. If you are ever tempted to spend too much time on your appearance, read St Teresa of Avila. Gifted with great physical beauty, she details in her autobiography the pitfalls of vanity she fell into in her younger years. She specifies the dangers and slippery slope that goes from beauty to vanity to the risk of losing chastity and one's honour. This will help you put things in perspective.[42]

The reason this is so important is that it would be easy for you to attract all kinds of men whom you do not want to be with, while the one you *do* want to be with you must attract in modest ways. So many women want men to admire their bodies, but in so doing they do not realise they degrade their natural feminine dignity and beauty, and instead appear cheap and vulgar. A virtuous man does not look for that in a woman, even though his fallen nature can certainly be allured by it. No, what he is looking for is natural grace in a good personality. If you have those, you will sooner or later get the right kind of attention from the right kind of man. *Favour is deceitful, and beauty is vain: the woman that feareth the Lord, she shall be praised.*[43]

The Objective Norm of Modesty

Now coming to some particulars regarding dress, this should be the overarching principle: any clothing that draws attention to any part of your body other than your face is immodest, and if a man takes interest in any other part of your body than your face, it means that he is interested in you for the wrong reasons. If you dress modestly, you are telling him that you have much more to offer than your body. You want him to appreciate you as a gifted person, not a physical trophy to be conquered. In other words, you conceal your body not because it is bad, but because it is so very good. By concealing it, you reveal your true dignity. The dress you described in your previous letter was too short at the bottom and at the top. It drew attention to your flesh in an inappropriate way. That is why you felt so bad.

You asked about dresses that flow down to the ankles and the wrists. I will be honest and say that it would make me happy to know that you are dressed that way. There is no more beautiful sight on earth, admirable to behold. Modest dress was a gift of God to the world after Original Sin,[44] for it allows a man to admire beauty in a woman without the risk of any unbecoming thoughts for her. If you ever have the opportunity to read about or to see documentaries on the way women dressed in former ages, all that went into preparing them for their daily duties, the noble gracefulness manifested in what they wore and everything they did, inspiring even all their movements, by all means study it well. Never forget that every woman is destined to be a spouse, a mother, a queen. The sight of a beautifully and modestly dressed woman warms the heart of every good man and fills it with wholesome thoughts, for the appeal is to all that is noble and generous in his own heart. Such a woman commands respect and trust.

But do you *have* to dress that way? Of course not. Dresses do not have to reach the ankles, but they do need to cover the knees when you are sitting, nor should you have to pull and stretch the skirt to make sure it does—that would be a sign that it is far too short. It does not have to cover the entire arm to the wrist. However it must cover the shoulders and should reach down to the elbow. Remember also how I wrote earlier that when it comes to dress, it is not just about hiding the skin, that is to say the external surface of the body, but also about hiding its form, its shape. An outfit that perfectly fits the body, even though it hides all the skin, such as a skin-tight form-fitting dress or skin-tight leggings—very common today—, is nonetheless immodest for the reason that the intimate shape of the body is on exhibit.

You might be wondering if the Church has ever given any guidelines on what is considered to be modest? She has indeed. On January 12, 1930, by mandate of Pope Pius XI, the Sacred Congregation of the Council sent to all bishops of the world a note directing them to insist on a number of prescriptions concerning modesty. They carry with them the specific weight of having been the only official declaration of the Church in this realm: "A dress cannot be called decent which is cut deeper than two fingers breadth under the pit of the throat, which does not cover the arms at least to the elbows, and scarcely reaches a bit beyond the knee. Furthermore, dresses of transparent material are improper".[45]

Here and there you will find people contending that these norms were established for a particular case, but in reality they are for all women in all countries, and were relayed at the time by bishops around the world. They have never been revoked. Furthermore, they simply express the requirements of dress in fallen human nature, which is the same in every clime, and as such, by their very nature are universally valid.

People base their whole lives on norms in one form or another. Norms guide the way we build our houses and drive our cars, the space we have to work in and the way we take our money out of the bank. There are standard colours and sizes, trademarks which establish standards of quality. We have standards of manners and of politeness directing us in the most minute details. At every turn one is confronted with standards. Why would the virtue of modesty be denied the right to be regulated and protected by objective and verifiable standards?

The Vessel of Life

You may be wondering why the "two fingers breadth under the pit of the throat". Well, Amanda, first of all, it is not helpful for any man to see a woman's décolletage. Secondly, God has made woman in such a wonderful way that when she becomes a mother she can nurse her own children with her own milk. This is proper to woman and a sign of her unique capacity to give and nurture infant life. It is therefore a sign of her dignity. But you need to know also that this area of the female body is a source of great attraction and curiosity for men.

This attraction can sometimes become perverse as the following example shows. The annals of the martyrdom of St Agatha tell us that the cruel tyrant ordered her breasts to be amputated. It is not a unique episode, to be true. This horrendous torture was inflicted on numerous holy women martyrs. But the amputation of a woman's breasts is not just an act of unspeakable cruelty, it is also an act of sacrilege, for it is to attack a woman precisely in her most noble capacity of motherhood. It is to profane the vessel of life. St Agatha's scathing reproach to the tyrant says it all. "Are you not ashamed to amputate in a woman what you yourself sucked in your own mother?" Her words are a remonstrance to any man who profanes the female body by trying to see what should remain hidden. So, keep in mind that to highlight that part of the body can precisely arouse in men an urge to see more.

There is a story about Pope St John XXIII in the days when he was still a cardinal. He was invited to a banquet and was sitting next to a woman who was wearing a low-cut dress. At the time of the dessert, he took an apple and offered it to her. The woman thanked him and asked if there was any particular reason for giving her the apple. He said, "Well, yes, there is, Madame. It was when Eve ate the apple that she realised she was naked". It was a humorous and not indelicate way of pointing out the immodesty of her dress.

We sometimes see women wearing low-cut blouses or dresses that seem designed to keep them from suffering from the heat. Well, sometimes modesty demands that one suffer a bit from the heat, for the good of the soul supersedes that of the body. St Thomas Aquinas teaches: "The good of our soul is more important than that of our body; and we have to prefer the spiritual welfare of our neighbour to our bodily comforts".[46]

In this context, I think it appropriate to add a word about breast-feeding. This maternal gesture, which is a vital and intimate moment between mother and babe, should be avoided in public, or if in a particular situation cannot be avoided, should be done as discreetly as possible with appropriate veiling of breast and babe. The reason is simply that it is not proper for a woman to bare her breasts in the presence of others, especially men, other than her husband.

Heels, Cosmetics and Other Adornments

The question of high heels requires a more nuanced answer. The reason many women wear heels is to appear more elegant. The problem is that this elegance comes at a price, for in most cases, high heels force a woman to walk with the chest protruding forward, the backside protruding backwards and an exaggerated sway of the hips—all of which increase the curves of the feminine physique that have a very strong sexual appeal to men, thus attracting their gaze to those parts of the body.[47] There are numerous studies that have confirmed this, and it is evidenced by the way high heels are marketed in advertising and fashion campaigns. Another disconcerting confirmation comes from certain developments in the field of plastic surgery, which was originally made to correct deformities and defects, and which has in recent years seen an exponential increase in procedures which are aimed at the enlargement precisely of both these focal points, the curves of the female body.⁴⁸ The fact that high heels result in a similar effect is a sad reality, that every Christian woman needs to be aware of, lest she unintentionally appeal to this base male instinct through her dress or comportment. To conclude then, if wearing heels is not in itself necessarily immodest, the effects produced by them, depending on the rest of the ensemble, can certainly be immodest.

You also asked about using makeup. As long as you do so "soberly and moderately and not excessively, shamelessly, and immodestly",⁴⁹ it is acceptable. Some women seem to put so much time and energy into making themselves so strikingly beautiful that the head of every man on the street will turn and gawk when they pass. That is vain and sinful. Use a little makeup, especially if you have some facial faults, but without losing too much time in front of the mirror.⁵⁰ As for styling your hair, of course. You do not have to let it flow freely.

Regarding your question about a woman dressing to please her husband, it is true that St Thomas says as much. However, this obviously means *within the bounds of Christian modesty,* as preference does not excuse sin. It does not mean she should dress immodestly because he likes it, for in that case she would be attractive for all men and not just for her husband, which is clearly reprehensible. St Thomas is referring to legitimate preferences in which a wife is commended for appearing attractive to her husband. So for example, if her husband prefers her hair to be styled in a certain way, or if he likes dresses of a certain cut or colour, or earrings of a certain kind, it is praiseworthy for the wife to please him in this.⁵¹

So Amanda, I hope I have sufficiently answered all your questions and any related ones that may have arisen. Before signing off, however, I would like to draw an important consequence from all this. Women who are given over to vanity and sensuality and who choose to dress immodestly, may imagine they are simply expressing themselves freely, when in reality they are slaves to the senses, always pandering to the exterior and forever remaining on the surface. These women, sadly, have no idea that there is another world of ineffable marvels that surpasses by far and cannot be compared to the world of the senses—the treasures of the spirit found in the interior life. The graces that are necessary to attain to these treasures are often only given by God when one makes a serious effort to live in a spirit of detachment from vain pleasures, and often the first step to be taken is modesty in dress and comportment, which does require a certain level of docility, sacrifice and mortification to please God.

If only these women knew what they are missing when they immerse themselves in the flesh and thereby lose the treasures of the spirit! It reminds me of St Augustine who after years of searching for the Lord, finally realised that he was on the outside, while God was on the inside: "Late have I loved Thee, O Beauty ever ancient, ever new, late have I loved Thee! Thou wert within me, but I was outside and it was there that I searched for Thee... Thou wert with me, but I was not with Thee".[52]

With that, Amanda, you have brief and concise guidelines to follow. If you observe them, you will be doing very well, you will be modest, you will please Our Lady very much, and you will bring much edification, peace and joy to the world.

With my blessing as always,

Your Father in Christ

FOURTH CORRESPONDENCE

Modesty in the Practicalities of
Daily Modern Life

When thou shalt see one naked,
cover her,
and despise not thy own flesh.

Isaiah 58:7

8 September 2023
Nativity of Our Lady

Dear Father,

I don't know how to thank you for the reply to my last letter. I showed it to Mum and she was over the moon with delight. So many things you mentioned, many of us women never think about, so your perspective, being that of a man and a priest, was most insightful and enlightening. Thank you so much for putting it so clearly, Father. On that note, I hope you don't mind, but I did have a few more specific questions to which I was again hoping you would provide some clear answers. I'm just going to dive straight into them.

One thing I noticed in all that you wrote is that you seem to assume that women wear dresses and skirts. You hardly ever mention trousers. Now, my mother never wears them, nor does my sister, but a lot of my friends do, and if I had to count the percentage of women I see out there, I'd say the immense majority wear trousers. I tried to apply to this the principles you gave me about modesty, and found myself wondering. I can see that very tight fitting trousers—especially the skintight leggings so many of my friends wear, that show too much of the shape of the lower body—are immodest. But what about normal trousers or jeans or even baggy trousers? Is it OK to wear those?

And also what about sports? Do I have to wear a skirt

when playing volleyball? It's not very practical, I must say! And what if I fall? It would be indecent...

And there is this really tough one: swimming and beaches? On the one hand, it seems that women should be able to go to the beach and swim. On the other hand, I'm not sure how all that fits in with what you have so eloquently said about modesty and chastity and occasions of sin? Is there some sort of "safe space" at the beach where men don't have temptations, or what? Or maybe, I thought that before going to the beach I could say a prayer so that any man who sees me will have the grace to contemplate feminine beauty without lust, but with detachment and as a gift of God. Is that appropriate?

As a family we only go to the beach for a few days during summer holidays, but there are also school swimming events at pools and, of course, swimming parties. Up to now, I have been to these, but I'm just wondering what to do.

I have a friend in America whose doctor ordered sunbathing to help her with some skin disease. Should she just let the disease kill her and die a victim of Christian modesty? What do you think, Father? Is it alright for women and girls to bathe in public and if so, what should they wear? Or does it matter?

Sorry if I'm asking so many questions! I just don't want to offend our Lord nor be an obstacle to anyone. But I don't want to be scrupulous either.

With gratitude as always,

Amanda

Clothing that cannot conceal the shape of the body is no more a covering. For such clothing, falling close to the body, takes its form more easily... As a result, the whole make of the body is visible to spectators, although they cannot see the body itself.

Clement of Alexandria

8 December 2023
Immaculate Conception of Our Lady

Dear Amanda,

Thank you once again for your openness and candid questions. Whoever seeks the truth finds it, and you are very good at seeking it, even though I have already given you some pretty demanding answers! I admire your perseverance. I'm also glad your mother liked my previous letters. Please pass on my regards to her.

Your questions now invite me to give some specific answers that some may find controversial. That's fine. It is good to have a healthy debate on these questions. I will endeavour, however, to back up my point of view with some solid reasoning and quotes from others so that you can see it is not just my personal opinion.

Women and Trousers

Tight-fitting trousers, both for men and for women, are obviously immodest for the reasons already mentioned. But what if they are loose-fitting? This is certainly better, but is it sufficient? If you read any of the literature on this subject among those who promote modesty in dress, you already know that there is quite a lot of debate going on as to whether or not it is fitting for women to wear trousers. There are many virtuous women who wear trousers habitually and see no issue with it at all. I will attempt here to give a fair answer to this question, but it is not easy to do so without appearing to be harsh or judgmental, so I ask you to bear patiently with me as I try to explain this as I see it.

Two very important realities undergird the entire question of whether or not women should wear trousers, and the answer we give will depend upon understanding them properly. The majority of women have never had them explained to them, and for that reason will need some time to assimilate them. Most men, however, who read what I am about to say, even if they have never been able to formulate it for themselves, will know instinctively that it is true.

Both these topics have to do with something mentioned earlier when I wrote of the way men are attracted to women. To use a modern expression taken from the computer world, men and women are "hardwired" differently, because in God's plan they are meant to fulfil specific and complementary roles. Man is the primary driver in the procreative act, and after he has shared his seed with his wife and new life is conceived, he must be the provider of the family and head of the household, which means going out and working in order to promote the family's interests. Woman receives her husband's initiative and becomes the vessel of new life, which she then nurtures with love and delicate attention, becoming the living heart of the home. She alone can do this. That is God's beautiful and wise plan for family life. It is precisely because of these fundamental differences in the male and female "hardwiring"—which are at once biological, physiological and psychological—that the nature of male and female perception and the effects of their clothing on the opposite sex differ immensely.

Furthermore, it is important to note that it was only once the feminist movement insisted on women being treated exactly like men and having all the same opportunities as men that we find them dressing like men. This is the true reason why trousers were first proposed as clothing for females: to promote the sameness of the sexes, thereby diminishing the unique dignity of the feminine role.

Here we are really at the heart of the entire question of modesty in dress and why it is, and always will be, more of a female question. I wrote in an earlier letter that man's attraction to woman is initially and principally visual and anatomical.[53] His instinct is to find a mate that will allow him to propagate the human species. In most cases, it is only later, as he matures, that his attraction becomes deeper and more emotional. Woman's attraction to man, on the other hand, is almost always initially emotional. She wants to be led and protected. When she looks at a man, she searches for signs of stability and the potential of being protected. The cases that lie outside this mean are often due to some trauma, either emotional or sexual in her childhood, or the practice of deviant sexual behaviour, which sadly is becoming more frequent. That is why, even though men and women both look for a potential mate, the response elicited, firstly through instinct, then tainted by concupiscence, is vastly different.

Differences in Visual Perception

Since, then, the sight of the female body, *of her flesh and her form,* is what principally attracts the male and what his eye instinctively seeks to discover—even before any act of the will intervenes—, any form of dress that draws attention to the female flesh or form is, of its very nature, going to tease that natural curiosity.

Now, the human eye naturally seeks to make sense of everything it sees. It groups things together into wholes, and follows the lead of lines and directions that it perceives in order to discover where they lead and what is behind them. If a line flows smoothly, for example, around the edges of an object such as a balloon, the eye follows it and the object is perceived *as a whole.* If a line, however, ends abruptly, the eye tends to stop there in order to observe and explore what it sees, and that object is perceived as a part rather than as a whole. We can all experience this when, for example, we see two sticks that are joined together: our eyes are naturally drawn to the area where they are joined; we want to figure out what is there and how it is held together at that spot.

Apply this now to the case of a woman wearing trousers. The male eye, which is already fascinated by the female body, is, of itself, drawn to her legs, the shape of which is made visible by the trousers. Seeing the legs then gives rise to an instinctive following their curve up to where the legs are joined, which is of course the most intimate part of her body. What that means in plain language is that when a woman is wearing trousers, a man's eyes are directed right to her private parts—both in the back and in the front. The trousers facilitate that natural flow of the eyes. Mind you, the same thing happens when a woman sees a man wearing trousers, but as we noted earlier, her instinct is not to focus on anatomy, and so it does not have the same effect as in a man.

So whenever a woman is wearing trousers, she can expect the eyes of the men who see her to go, as of themselves, to her most private area. A man's instinctive, built-in tendency to discover, explore and enter into a woman's physical intimacy is abetted by the sight of a woman wearing trousers. We must add, however, that there is nothing "dirty-minded" about this reflex—the angles automatically direct the eyes there. We must also repeat that this instinct, as we saw earlier, is deeply wounded by Original Sin. This does not let men off the hook. It means they must practice custody of the eyes, but sadly, few do. Men must form their will to cooperate with grace so as to not let wounded nature run its course, at least as far as thoughts are concerned.[54]

Apply this now to the case of a woman wearing a long dress or skirt. In this case, the man does not have this instinctive following the curve up between the legs, for the simple reason that he does not see the legs, as they are hidden by the dress; his eyes will then be inclined to follow the outside of the dress up to her face, and he sees, not a part of her anatomy, but a person, a woman, a human being; his eyes rest in the vision of that whole person, and his heart remains at peace in the calm, tranquil perception that he has seen a very beautiful sight, one that he wants instinctively to honour and not abuse.

When you place these principles of visual perception alongside the teaching of the Church on concupiscence, it is easy to understand why, since the dawn of history until very recently, it has always been unthinkable for women to wear trousers. This explains also why trousers in men, although of rather recent use in history, never encountered any such objection.

At the end of the day, even though this information may be confronting and uncomfortable, we are brought back to one of the points I mentioned when writing about the propriety of the veil: the female body is sacred, it is more sacred than the male, because it is the source and the guardian of life, and therefore needs to be protected by more ample clothing. This was seen across cultures around the world despite the modes of dress being so varied. It has little to do with culture and everything to do with the nature of reality.

Ideological Issues

If the first reason trousers are not advisable for women is anatomical, the second is more ideological; its effects are rooted, not so much in man's carnal arousal as in the woman's delicate and highly refined psyche.

The one who, as far as I know, has given the most incisive considerations on this is Cardinal Giuseppe Siri (1906-1989).[55] The overarching principle he explains this way: "The clothing a person wears conditions, determines and modifies that person's gestures, attitudes and behaviour, such that from merely being worn outside, clothing comes to impose a particular frame of mind inside". Based on this principle, he notes three main areas that are affected when a woman wears trousers like a man: the female psyche, the relationship of woman with her husband, and the effect on the children.

The first concern is that it changes woman's own psychology. Indeed, if she dresses like a man, her motive can only be that of imitating and even of competing with man whom she considers to be stronger, less tied down and more independent. Dressing like a man becomes the visible aid to being like a man, and by the very fact, she becomes less a woman. Furthermore, when a woman wears trousers, she tends to act and be treated like a man, her gestures and way of walk are less feminine (women are shown to sit and walk differently in skirts and in trousers), and she tends to confuse the roles of men and women. This is one of the main reasons for which God gave this command in the Old Testament: *A woman shall not be clothed with man's apparel neither shall a man use woman's apparel: for he that doeth these things is abominable before God* (Dt 22:5). It is also the reason for which some say that trousers on a woman are worse than a miniskirt, because while the miniskirt has a more immediate sensual attraction due to the degree of bare flesh visible so close to the intimate part of the body, trousers are ideological and attack the mind. The miniskirt can be linked to an increase of overtly sensual dressing and a monumental drop in the standards of modesty, but it is still essentially feminine. The adoption of trousers for women were, however, driven by the radical women's rights movement whose ideology and crusade rallied against the traditional female role in society as a mother and heavily encouraged the 'equality/sameness' of the sexes. This is at the crux of much of the social upheaval and war against woman and the family.

The second concern is the way it changes her relationship with her husband. Indeed, if she dresses like man and wants to compete with man, then the principle man in her life (her husband) cannot help but sense—even if he does not express it to himself this way—that he is not doing his job well enough, and consequently this can vitiate the relationship between the sexes which God saw as a complementarity and not a competition. Cardinal Siri goes so far as to say that "a woman wearing men's dress always more or less indicates her reacting to her femininity as though it were inferior (to masculinity) when in fact it is only diverse". This insidious mentality has grave adverse effects on woman but also on man. Men by nature are meant to lead, and so if a man's wife makes it clear that she wants to do the leading, the man, especially if he is less gifted than his wife, finds himself emasculated.

The third concern is that it affects the woman vis-à-vis her children by harming her dignity in their eyes. Indeed, from a very young age children are sensitive to the way their mother dresses. They sense that she is different from their father, but this needs to be confirmed by her apparel, that is to say, a more dignified, feminine and modest way of dressing. Seeing young mothers in shorts with their little children grabbing their legs is most unedifying. Worse, it lodges within the child's psyche that Mummy is not any different from Daddy or their friends. Some will object that when a mother has small children, if she is wearing a dress, there can be embarrassing and unedifying moments when the children will pull up her dress. This of course is true, but it is an extra reason why a *long* dress, and not just one down below the knees is preferable. But it is also true that the wearing of a dress dictates gestures and attitudes that are not required when wearing trousers or shorts and which of their very nature make for more dignity and honour in the way one does things, such as bending down the knees to attend to a child, instead of bowing over in an unseemly way in the presence of others.

This example is crucial for small children, for Christian modesty begins at that age. Children must be taught from a very tender age to be fully clothed in the presence of others and to never expose their body to others. Parents (and those who assist them) have a special responsibility to guard the modesty of children and to provide a good example. Parents must not allow them to run around half-naked. Those who do not take this responsibility seriously will have to answer to God for their conduct.

Pope Pius XII had these sober words to say to Christian mothers in particular, concerning both their own dress and that of their children: "The good of our soul is more important than the good of our body; and we have to prefer the spiritual welfare of our neighbour to our bodily comforts. If a certain kind of dress constitutes a grave and proximate occasion of sin, and endangers the salvation of your soul and others, it is your duty to give it up... O Christian mothers, if you knew what a future of anxieties and perils, of ill-guarded shame you prepare for your sons and daughters, imprudently getting them accustomed to live scantily dressed and making them lose the sense of modesty, you would be ashamed of yourselves and you would dread the harm you are making for yourselves, the harm which you are causing these children, whom Heaven has entrusted to you to be brought up as Christians."[56]

Dignity and Decorum

Now, let's look at the question of the trousers from another important perspective, namely that of dignity. Have you ever noticed what priests at the altar, magistrates in court, kings and queens in their regalia all have in common? They are wearing robes that flow and drape in a regal manner that is not form-fitting and that conceal rather than reveal the presence of the human being who present. This concealment plays a key role in stressing the dignity of their office. It means that when we are in their presence, we do not think so much of their merely mortal functions, but rather are drawn to focus on the elevated and sublime nature of what they symbolise. These roles all reveal and allude to the plan of God's eternal wisdom: the priest who takes the place of Christ on earth (*alter Christus*); the judge who dispenses justice; the political powers who rule for the common good as representatives of God; woman, the bearer and nurturer of new life and the vessel of God's love.

This is perhaps the most important reason for which a woman should always wear a dress or a skirt: it both adorns and safeguards her beautiful and delicate feminine dignity. Every woman is by nature equipped to be a mother, and a mother is, naturally speaking, the most dignified position on earth. By her very nature she contributes to society, either through the raising of children or through the feminine influence that speaks to the heart of all those around her. When a man sees a woman in a beautiful, long, modest dress, his reaction is instinctively one of reverence and honour as he finds himself in the presence of an awesome mystery that his nature tells him must be respected. Whereas immodest dress and trousers detract significantly from feminine dignity, a modest dress makes her look like a queen, so worthy of honour that to touch her, and even to have unbecoming thoughts about her, would be a sacrilege.

Cardinal Siri concluded his thoughts with these strong words: "Experience teaches us that when woman is de-feminised, defences are undermined and weakness increases... The changing of feminine psychology does fundamental and—in the long run—irreparable damage to the family, to conjugal fidelity, to human affections and to human society. True, the effects of wearing unsuitable dress are not all to be seen within a short time. But one must think of what is being slowly and insidiously worn down, torn apart, perverted. Is any satisfying reciprocity between husband and wife imaginable, if feminine psychology be changed? Or is any true education of children imaginable, which is so delicate in its procedure, so woven of imponderable factors in which the mother's intuition and instinct play the decisive part in those tender years? What will these women be able to give their children when they will so long have worn trousers that their self-esteem is determined more by their competing with the men than by their functioning as women?... To sum up, wherever women wear men's dress, it is to be considered a factor, over the long term, in disintegrating human order".

One of the gravest effects of "disintegrating human order" that is before us today is gender confusion. With the loss of feminine dignity and the effect of this loss on the heart and emotions of those under her care, one can only wonder whether the unisex forms of dress that have become common are not part of the problem. Actually, this is something that has been suggested by professional psychologists. Dutch Catholic psychologist Gerard van den Aardweg, who had decades of successful therapeutic experience with persons experiencing same-sex attraction (SSA), notes that in cultures (even the most primitive and pagan) where the clear distinction is made between boys and girls, homosexuality is very rare, if not non-existent. As part of his therapy in treating such individuals, this orthodox Catholic psychologist advised women affected by SSA to make an effort to dress in as feminine a way as possible with a nice gown or other typical women's dress. He also stated that "the ideology that obliterates sex roles is so unnatural that future generations will undoubtedly see it as a perversion of a decadent culture".[57]

Those are some very sobering remarks from someone who has such long experience in this domain. Our world urgently needs to take them to heart. Clearly, SSA and gender confusion are very complex issues, the causes of which are multifactorial. Dr Aardweg is well aware of them, but his remarks on the specific area of dress are certainly worth considering. His experience as a psychologist showed him that there are many differences in the way that boys and girls are brought up. If these are not respected, the door is open to SSA and gender confusion. Furthermore, Dr Aardweg noticed positive changes in women struggling with SSA when they did start dressing in a feminine manner.

Exceptions

After all this, you might be wondering if there are ever any circumstances in which trousers are acceptable. Well, as you know, in some work contexts women sometimes don't really have a choice, but that also brings up the question of whether or not women should be involved in those kinds of work at all—but let's save that one for another conversation... I do know a practicing female doctor who has gradually shifted to always wearing a dress at work. It has not created any problems for her, but interestingly has spurred a number of questions about her attire, giving her the opportunity to explain the reasons for Christian modesty. Another young woman who is a teacher of primary school children and who shifted to only wearing beautiful feminine attire to school was amazed to find her little students of age 7 and 8, both boys and girls, notice, comment, and compliment her on her feminine clothing. Both these women are examples of how small changes can bring about profound effects on those who are in one's scope of influence and care. That is the way we will reconquer the culture—one by one!

There are occasions in which wearing a dress would be dangerous. If you have to do work on a ladder, wear some baggy trousers and make sure you have a long blouse or tunic that extends well past your hips and provides sufficient coverage of the posterior. Do the same if you have to work around dangerous machinery in which a dress could be caught, and you or others could be seriously injured.

In defence of women wearing trousers, people frequently bring up the example of St Joan of Arc who, when sent by God to lead the French armies, surrounded by men with whom she had to share living quarters, donned male military apparel and armour, and later when in prison, refused to change into a dress that was given her because she knew that the soldiers would take advantage of her. Let's be clear: St Joan cannot be used in defence of women wearing trousers. The military apparel, especially with the addition of full body metal armour and plates, would have certainly not displayed the form of her body or highlighted intimate areas. You can be sure she would not have been prancing around in tight leggings nor leading an army to battle in them![58]

Sportswear

You are probably aware that female sports were not common until modern times. The obvious reason is that women have babies and it is somewhat difficult to have babies and play sports at the same time. But what about women who are not mothers? As long as it is understood that maternity is a married woman's highest calling and should never be shunned because of sports, there is no objection, as such, to most women's sports.[59] There is, however, and a serious one, with regard to what women wear—or rather, don't wear—while playing.

When women's sports started to become popular, there were strict rules concerning their appearance. If you look at early 20th century female tennis players, for example, you will see them wearing long skirts and long sleeves on the court. As public fashions evolved, so did female sportswear, and nowadays, they often appear less clothed than the men, wearing shorts or miniskirts which leave much of their thighs visible and sometimes display bare shoulders and backs; this is certainly not acceptable. A woman's thighs, shoulders and back should never be on public display. Indeed, Holy Scripture speaks of such a display to be shameful in a woman: *Uncover thy shame, strip thy shoulder, make bare thy legs, pass over the rivers. Thy nakedness shall be discovered, and thy shame shall be seen.*[60]

My opinion, and that of many women who have tried it, is that it is perfectly feasible to dress modestly and play most sports. For example, it is acceptable to wear tracksuit trousers or leggings under a skirt that reaches the knees, along with a loose blouse that goes down below the waist. This safeguards modesty (hiding the form), while providing for covering in the case of a fall or simply the gestures required to play the sport.

There is another reason, which might surprise you, for which I know for a fact that most sports are quite possible while wearing a skirt. In traditional monasteries, it is common for monks and nuns to play sports such as volleyball, basketball, soccer, hiking, and even cycling while wearing their habits. There is no danger in this once you get used to it. (Of course, if you do wear a skirt to cycle, be sure to wear leggings or a tracksuit!) The same principle goes for riding horse back, running, skating, and many other sports.

This is also in keeping with the instructions given by Pope Pius XI: "Let parents keep their daughters from public gymnastic games and contests; but if their daughters are compelled to attend such exhibitions, let them see that they are fully and modestly dressed. Let them never permit their daughters to don immodest garb... [I]n gymnastic exercises and deportment, special care must be had of Christian modesty in young women and girls, which is so gravely impaired by any kind of exhibition in public".[61] In other words, sport should not become an idol, an end in itself, which justifies women appearing in public half-naked. Modesty in dress is required even there.

If it is objected that in some places it would be very hot, let's remember that a fundamental principle about clothing is that it came as the result of sin, and therefore has a certain penitential character about it. We should not be afraid of a little heat. By the way, the hottest countries are those in which the most clothing is worn, for the simple reason that the body must be protected from an aggressive sun. We see this in hot desert areas where people dress in long, light coloured (to reflect the sun), full coverage loose garments made of natural fibres such as cotton. This allows airflow that ensures any perspiration will create a cooling effect.

I remember one summer day walking down a street in my monastic habit and a fellow remarked to me that I must be hot. I replied: "Yeah, but it's hotter in Hell!" He got the point. If you have gotten the gist of what I have been saying over and over again, you are fully aware now that when it comes to modesty in dress, what we are really dealing with is mortal sin, and mortal sin sends souls to Hell. Better suffer from a little heat here and avoid eternal fire.

Swimming Suits

First of all, I know this is not a problem for you,—it gave me great satisfaction to read that you would not be caught dead in one!—but it surely is for many of your friends, so let's begin by categorically ruling out and vigorously condemning the bikini, for which there is literally no justification whatsoever. Far from respecting the measure of modesty, it is the epitome of extreme and grave immodesty. Though it wrongly satisfies the legal requirement for not being naked (thankfully there are still laws in most places banning public nudity), it does not stand up to the requirements of reason. Let's be clear: to wear a bikini is to be naked, for the simple reason that the very design leaves no option to the eye but to see the missing parts.

A simple observation will prove my point. We all know by experience that whatever stands out visually will capture and hold our attention first. For example, if we have a group of ten people dressed in black and one in the middle dressed in red, it is the one in red who attracts most of the attention; the red one simply stands out. The first point of interest grabs our attention. Applying this to the bikini, when a woman's naked body has only two tiny pieces of clothing which cover the intimate parts but carefully and intentionally reveal their shape, the eye of the beholder is, of necessity, drawn precisely to those intimate parts. Those tiny pieces of clothing are therefore not designed to clothe at all, but to reveal, by drawing all the attention to that area. This being the case, the viewer is seeing those areas as objects—this explains why the beholder tends to objectify the woman—rather than part of the whole person.[62] It is therefore clear that the bikini is designed not to clothe but to undress. In other words, it does not qualify as clothing at all and seems to have been designed to intentionally arouse lust in men. As an aside, if the bikini were helpful for swimming, professional swimmers would wear them, but they don't. On this topic, when you go shopping for clothes, remember this fundamental point: clothing is about concealing. If you find yourself asking how much you can get away with in terms of what you reveal, you are not really looking for clothing at all, but for nudity.

Combine the natural reflexes and instincts which drive male perception with the woundedness of Original Sin and the subsequent triggering of concupiscence, and you are left with an obvious conclusion: extreme forms of immodesty, instead of clothing a person, actually unclothe them in the eyes of the beholder. Such a lack of modesty can only then be a cause of many mortal sins that could be prevented if the most basic requirements of modesty were respected.

Such deleterious effects have also been demonstrated through secular research such as this study performed at Princeton University in 2008, which revealed that when men see a woman wearing a bikini, the region of the brain associated with tool use lights up.[63] Furthermore, men are more likely to associate images of such women with first-person action verbs such as "I push, I grasp, I handle, I control, I grab". In other words, these men saw women as sexually inviting, but they were not thinking about their persons at all, only about their bodies seen as objects for pleasure. It's even worse when you find out that the pictures presented to the men in this study were of headless women in bikinis. In other words, the face, which is the image of the person and the way they relate to the world and are respected as humans, was irrelevant.[64] All that mattered was their body to be used as an object. Conclusion? If a female does not want to be seen as a tool, a toy or a piece of meat, then the bikini is certainly not the way to go.

Now let's go back to Genesis and remember that Adam and Eve covered themselves with fig leaves which God said were not sufficient. The fig leaves are reminiscent of undergarments that adhere to the bare flesh, but are not sufficient garb to appear in public (Adam and Eve must have appeared very much like most people do today on our beaches!). Being expelled from the Garden of Eden was like leaving the privacy of their bedroom: they now needed proper clothes. In other words, there are certain forms of clothing that are not acceptable in public, even if they cover the most intimate parts of the body. It would be a disgrace, the equivalent of being naked. Would you walk down the street with only your underwear? On this note, it comes as no surprise that when the first bikini was introduced to the public on 5 July 1946, the designer, unable to find a runway model who would accept to wear and advertise it, had to hire a stripper—no other woman would accept. Even the models in those days had enough modesty to not appear in public in their underwear![65] How things have changed!

Unfortunately, the common one-piece swimming suits available today are for the most part almost just as immodest as the bikini, most of them offering no coverage at all below the pelvis, and being quite revealing at the top; furthermore they are designed to show the exact curves of the entire body, which of itself, as we saw earlier, is gravely immoral. It is possible, however, to find some that are acceptable, covering most of the body.[66]

In 1954 Pope Pius XII issued a letter on modesty which it is worthwhile to quote here: "Everyone knows that during the summer months particularly, things are seen here and there which are certain to prove offensive to anyone who has retained some respect and regard for Christian virtue and human modesty. On the beaches, in country resorts, almost everywhere, on the streets of cities and towns, in private and public places, and, indeed, often in buildings dedicated to God, an unworthy and indecent mode of dress has prevailed. Because of this, the young particularly, whose minds are easily bent towards vice, are exposed to the extreme danger of losing their innocence, which is, by far, the most beautiful adornment of mind and body. Feminine adornment, if it can be called adornment, feminine clothing, 'if that can be called clothing which contains nothing to protect either the body or modesty' (*Seneca*), are at times of such a nature that they seem to serve lewdness rather than modesty. What we are discussing here is obviously most serious, since it vitally concerns not only Christian virtue but also the health and vigour of human society. Well did not the ancient poet say of this matter: 'Vice necessarily follows upon public nudity' (*Ennius*)".[67] When we add to this what the Venerable Archbishop Fulton Sheen said about nudity being the mark of the demonic, we can see clearly where this movement comes from and where it leads.

It should be pointed out too that ordinarily men are dressed more modestly on our beaches than women. True, they are bare-backed most of the time, but this is culturally acceptable for men, even though I am of the mind that it should be avoided unless there are only men around. But you would rarely find a man wearing the revealing type of swimsuit (what are called speedos) that most female suits provide. More generally, it is shocking that when you meet people on the streets or on hikes, men almost always have long shorts down to the knees, while the women frequently seem to have to exhibit their thighs—and as much of them as they can possibly manage…

Fig leaves are not enough! To cover the bare minimum in public is like being naked; in a way it is worse, because it can arouse the passions even more by the "hide and seek" mentality it encourages. When prostitutes "advertise" themselves, they do not walk around naked. Sometimes they might even be hard to distinguish from modest women, but most of the time, they will dress in ways that entice the eyes to certain parts of the body that are more attractive to men. They do not show their hidden parts, but the way they dress and act invites men to want to see them.

It's an unspoken message that says: "you can see more if you want it". I definitely do not intend to imply that whenever a woman dresses in such a way she is playing the harlot. What I want to get across to you, since I have a responsibility for your dear soul, is that regardless of intentions, there are ways of dressing which, objectively speaking, send that message.

A Modest Solution

So what to do? At the risk of sounding old-fashioned (anything wrong with that?), I contend that early 20th century swimming attire is appropriate. The women wore long shorts at least to the knees, and shirts with sleeves to the elbow. The men did pretty much the same thing. When you see photos of those days, you can't help but admire the propriety and dignity of it all. Furthermore, most bathing was done either as a family or with men and women bathing separately. If everyone respected those rules, it would be possible to go to the beach without being in a constant occasion of mortal sin. But you must remember that even baggy swimming gear, when wet, clings to the skin and looks tight, leaving the body shape to appear. That is why it is good to have a skirted swimsuit to preserve not only modesty but also femininity. If everyone did this, you could go to any beach, but sadly, most women are almost naked on the beach nowadays, so I'm afraid I must strongly advise against going there unless you can find a spot in which one is not constantly in the occasion of sin. If not, you need to forego.

I have nonetheless been greatly pleased to learn that there are growing numbers of women who would never be seen in one of the immodest outfits mentioned earlier. I was also pleasantly surprised to learn recently that there are local pools that reserve certain hours for female bathing only. This denotes respect for women and provides them with an opportunity to bathe without being watched by men. It also proves that there are many more women who want to dress modestly than you might think by walking down the street in the summer. The numbers are growing. Common sense always makes a comeback.

You asked if the beach is a "safe-space" where men have no temptations. I think what I have already said answers that. Think for a minute. What you asked would mean that as soon as a woman sets foot on a beach, even though she is virtually naked and might even, without any reprehensible intentions, assume suggestive postures which would be condemned in any other place as downright seduction, temptation in men suddenly diminishes, sleeps, or perhaps dies. But if the same woman in the same attire walks down the street or knocks at the door of his house, he is supposed to somehow recover the effects of Original Sin? I hope you see the nonsense.

You also asked if it would be OK to pray before going to the beach so that men won't be tempted when seeing you. That is a praiseworthy thing to do, but it does not dispense you from dressing modestly! No, there is no place where men are not tempted by a beautiful woman. The devil does not sleep, and even when the flesh appears to be dormant, it never dies until it is dead. Forget not King David. He was a saint, a man according to the Heart of God. And yet, it took only a bathing beauty, whom he spied from the roof of his palace, to smite him down. The sight of this woman (who by the way was not necessarily entirely naked) so kindled in his heart the fire of concupiscence, as to lead him to the double crime of adultery and murder. Today bathing beauties continue to be an alluring bait dangled before the eyes of fallen men plagued with concupiscence, and who, like the fly drawn by the fire, are scorched to death by the poison of lust that is injected into their hearts by the exhibition of flesh. For good men, the practical consequence of this is that most beaches are off limits. The immodest, impure fashions prevent them from enjoying the innocent pleasures which a beach could afford.

Personal Modesty and Courtesy for Others

A final and more general word on this account is that modesty is usually referred to with regard to the way people appear in public, but there is also a personal modesty when we are utterly alone. It is not appropriate even when alone to be entirely unclothed (except of course when taking a bath or showering). We must always have the sense of the presence of God and His angels who surround us at all times. Even though they are obviously not tempted by the naked human body, we should, out of respect for their majestic presence, humbly appear before them clothed not only with the garment of grace, but also with the garments of human dignity, for our body, although created by God and very beautiful, is nevertheless, and until the final resurrection, wounded by sin and concupiscence, ever inclined to seek its own pleasure instead of the will of God. St Thomas has some very insightful words on this: "In the state of corrupt nature, man needs grace to heal his nature in order that he may entirely abstain from sin. And in the present life this healing is wrought in the mind, the carnal appetite being not yet restored".[68] In other words, if by cooperation with God's grace it is possible to avoid all mortal sins, the complete healing of the flesh won't take place until after the final resurrection. Hence, even great saints still have involuntary movements of the flesh and can thus commit venial sins in this realm. This is another reason for modesty in dress: we do not want to prevent only mortal sins, but even venial ones. Modesty in dress goes a long way towards that.

One day there was a priest who was travelling with an older couple when they stopped in to pay a brief visit to their son and his family. It was hot, and the children were in the pool. The parents called them to come and say hello to the priest. The older lady, a solid Catholic formed in the true ways of modesty, immediately saw the unbecomingness of the situation and promptly stepped in while her adolescent granddaughter was still at a good distance, and had her cover herself with a towel. It was the perfect example of a grandmother saving a situation that her son and daughter-in-law, sadly, had not even noticed, sparing a man of God the awkward situation of having to greet a barely dressed female.

There are also situations where women at a particular gathering will dress more modestly out of respect for a priest they know will be present. This is a very good instinct in Christian women who should be more careful around priests or religious, for even the best of them are frail men, and you do not want to be, even inadvertently, the cause of even a venial sin in them. However, out of Christian charity this attitude should be extended to any man. Every Christian woman should want to avoid being an occasion even of unbecoming thoughts or venial sins of frailty in this realm. But that of course requires a profound love for chastity. A woman who does not have that love, will often be oblivious to her own impurities and careless of causing them in others, while a woman who, through prayer and self-denial, discovers the price and beauty of being chaste, instinctively covers herself in a dignified way, thereby finding peace in her soul, a peace that then emanates from her very person and has a profound effect on those around her.

As for sunbathing, if a doctor prescribes it, you will comply by doing so in a closed space. It does not have to be done on a beach. However, if you live in Australia, I doubt such a prescription will be forthcoming!

With my blessing,

Your Father in Christ

FINAL EXHORTATION

An Urgent Letter of Appeal to All
Spiritual Daughters

Up with us then at last, for the Scripture arouseth us, saying: It is now the hour for us to rise from sleep (Rom 13:11).

Rule of St Benedict, Prologue

25 December 2023
Christmas Day

My Daughter,

I have been thinking of you since my last letter, and on this day of Our Lord's birth of the Virgin, wanted to send you a follow up letter of encouragement. You are no doubt wondering at this stage how you will have the strength to put into practice all the things we have discussed. Even more, you will be trying to figure out how to influence other women, many of whom are, so it seems, in another universe when it comes to modesty. You may be tempted to think we are fighting a lost battle, that the Pandora's box has been opened and there is nothing we can do to close it, that we are being helplessly swept away by a merciless current. Well, remember that only what's dead flows with the current. Remember also this: "Nobody made a greater mistake than he who did nothing because he could do only a little".[69] By dressing modestly yourself, you may seem to be doing little, but it is little by little that we will restore Christian morals.

Besides, we have a lot more going for us than they do. True, the spirit of evil has succeeded in persuading too many women that they can dress and undress as they please ("my body, my choice!" goes the slogan). There is, however, a growing number of women—and the media does not give them much attention—who, like you, have come to know the truth, and sincerely want to be part of the rebuilding of a truly Christian society, which has as one of its essential foundation stones the recovery of Christian modesty in churches, in the home, at schools, in the workplace, on the street, at the gym, on the beaches—everywhere.

A great movement for this restoration is already beginning. Remember that Our Lord converted the world with just twelve men. Twelve good women are enough to convert the world to modesty if they truly set out to do it, with the grace of God. Recall too yet another word of G.K. Chesterton speaking of the "democracy of the dead", meaning that when we take polls to find out how many are on our side, we need to count the generations that have gone before us. When we do this, we notice right away that those in favour of modesty by far outnumber those who have caved in to modern quasi-nude fashions. We have all of history on our side! You also have many saintly models to look up to and turn your attention with particular devotion, placing yourself under their patronage. I mentioned earlier St Agatha. Let's consider a few others.

In the acts of the martyrdom of St Agnes, there is a moving page that tells how, in an attempt to break her resolve of fidelity to Christ, the tyrant ordered her to be stripped, her virginal body exposed and violated. Sadly, it was not an uncommon tactic among the pagan persecutors towards virtuous young Christian women; they understood better than most Christians today the link between purity of faith and purity of morals. If they could take away chastity, they thought, the faith would fall likewise. It was then that took place a stupendous miracle: her beautiful hair, which was of normal length for a girl of twelve, instantly grew down to her feet, covering her entire body, sheltering her from the lustful gaze of the mob. This astounding miracle shows us how God watches over His saints. It also shows us His love for purity, His love for virginity and the importance He attaches to its first safeguard, namely modest clothing. It will encourage you to have recourse to St Agnes in your efforts to reconvert the world to sanity.

Consider also the example of St Lucy. Like Agnes, her torturers wanted to deprive her not only of her faith but also of her virginity. To this end, the wicked judge ordered her to be taken to an execrable place where she would lose her virginity, in other words, to a brothel. Here too, an amazing miracle took place: Lucy, the slender young woman, became immobile—she could not be budged! To pull her, the torturers had recourse to every means at their disposal, including the strongest men they could find and even several yoke of oxen. Nothing availed. She remained firm like a pillar, the Holy Spirit Himself giving her superhuman strength. The example of St Lucy will help you when others try to persuade you to go along with the crowd, or to give up because no one is following you. No, stand firm, Amanda, and you will see the Holy Spirit in Person intervene to make you stronger than all the legions of Hell combined!

Another martyr of the early Christian era I would like to offer as a model is St Perpetua. It is recounted, in the acts of her martyrdom with St Felicity and others, that, as part of her torment in the amphitheatre at Carthage, she was thrown into the air by a wild heifer. When she fell to the ground and realised that her tunic had been ripped, leaving her bare thigh visible, her first thought and action was to pull down her tunic in such a way as to cover her nakedness. This admirable woman thought more of Christian modesty in that hour of torture than of her excruciating pain and her imminent death. Amazingly too, she was concerned with being beautiful for the Lord, and so she asked for a pin to fasten her untidy hair, thinking it not right that a martyr should die with her hair in disorder, lest she might seem to be mourning in her hour of triumph. May St Perpetua always inspire you with her moving example of true Christian beauty and modesty!

Closer to us, think of St Maria Goretti, the young Italian girl who, when solicited by a boy several years older and much stronger than her to consent to his shameful advances, firmly rejected them, telling him: "No, you will go to Hell!" She paid dearly for her heroic virtue. Beside himself with passion, he stabbed her again and again with a knife, leaving her half dead. She would agonise for two full days before rendering her pure soul to God, but not before forgiving her assassin, Alessandro Serenelli, who would do penance and eventually be present in Rome when she was canonised fifty years later. Alessandro would write a beautiful letter of testimony on his conversion due to St Maria's intercession, in which we can read these words: "My behaviour was influenced by print, mass-media and bad examples which are followed by the majority of young people without even thinking. And I did the same. I was not worried. There were a lot of generous and devoted people who surrounded me, but I paid no attention to them because a violent force blinded me and pushed me toward a wrong way of life." This episode shows both the lethal power of lust and lustful propaganda by the press, but also the superior power of the Holy Spirit who strengthens weak and fragile souls to offer their lives for purity. May St Maria Goretti share with you her love for modesty and purity, even unto death were it to lead there.

Such is the power of the Holy Spirit, my Daughter, at work in His saints. All He asks for is a bit of good will, and a great desire to save souls. If you have those and give yourself to Him, one step at a time you will progress to true sanctity, and in so doing you will influence many more women and girls than you can imagine.

These examples and many others also show us that we are indeed engaged in a fierce battle. The enemy of our human nature does not hesitate to use violence and death, just as he did against Christ Our Lord. And yet, we know that it is in dying that we are born to eternal life. Fear nothing. Fear no one. You may be opposed by your family or closest friends. You might even be put to scorn by priests or nuns. Fear not, but stand firm!

If you do, we have every reason to be optimistic about the future. You will continue to reconquer the lost ground, one step at a time. What we need is a new crusade for purity and Christian modesty... My Dear Daughter, will you take up the challenge?

With my blessing,

Your Father in Christ

Notes

1. *Sensus fidei*: sense or understanding of the truths of the faith.

2. G. K. Chesterton, *What's Wrong with the World*, Part III, Chapter 10: The Higher Anarchy.

3. 1 Corinthians 11:1-16.

4. And this regardless of whether the Blessed Sacrament is in the tabernacle or not, even though it is especially required when approaching the altar for Holy Communion.

5. Some argue that since the 1983 Code abolished the 1917 Code, any prescriptions that were not resumed in the later code are abolished as well. This is flimsy canonical reasoning, since legitimate customs stand unless they are specifically abrogated or fall into universal disuse. Furthermore one of the principles that governed the 1983 revision was simplification. Many things were omitted in order to make for a corpus of laws that was easier to use. A point in case is the canon that forbade enrolment in Freemasonry. The mention was omitted in the new code, but the Holy See has recalled on at least two occasions that such enrolment is still forbidden by the very nature of Freemasonry, which is incompatible with the Catholic faith. *Mutatis mutandis*, the situation with the veil is similar, but the case is even more clearcut: by the very nature of the apostolic precept and the universal custom of the Church from antiquity, it is not required that the custom be recalled for it to be valid, even though it is to be hoped that it one day will be.

6. Cf. Eph 5:28-33.

7. St Elizabeth of the Trinity, *Heaven In Faith*, Second Day.

8. A sacrilege is the abuse of a sacred person, object or place. Since a church is a place consecrated to God, the giving of scandal through immodest dress while there takes on the added gravity of a sacrilege.

9. I knew a priest in my youth who was clear on this point: if the gowns were not modest, the wedding would not take place. To avoid this, it has been suggested that priests should have a photo album with acceptable gowns so that young brides-to-be can choose well in advance one that is modest, instead of putting the priest before the *fait accompli* on the day of the wedding.

10. "The parish priest and especially the preacher, when occasion arises, should according to the words of the Apostle Paul (2 Tim 4:2) insist, argue, exhort and command that feminine garb be based on modesty and womanly ornament be a defence of virtue. Let them likewise admonish parents to cause their daughters to cease wearing indecorous dress... Girls and women dressed immodestly are to be debarred from Holy Communion and from acting as sponsors at the Sacraments of Baptism and Confirmation; further, if the offence be extreme, they may even be forbidden to enter the church" (Decree of the Congregation of the Council, by the mandate of Pope Pius XI, 12 January 1930).

11. Gn 3:7.

12. Cf. G. K. Chesterton, *Orthodoxy*, ch. 2.

13. Gn 3:7.

14. Ibid.

15. Gn 3:21.

16. 1 Pet 3:7.

17. See St Thomas Aquinas, *Summa Theologiæ*, IIa-IIae, q. 151, a. 1.

18. Bishop Athanasius Schneider's definition in the catechism *Credo*, q. 525.

19. Cf. *Summa Theologiæ*, IIa-IIae, q. 160, a. 1.

20. Wisdom 4:1.

21. Gal 5:22-23.

22. *Catechism of the Catholic Church*, 2521.

23. 2 Sam 11:2.

24. Mt 5:28.

25. Gen 4:9.

26. Mt 22:39.

27. Ecclesiasticus [Sirach] 9:5, 9.

28. Eph. 5:3.

29. St Francis de Sales, *Introduction to the Devout Life*, Part 3, ch. 3.

30. 1 Cor 3:16-17.

31. Pius XII, July 17, 1954.

32. Mt 7:13-14.

33. G. K. Chesterton, *The Shadow of the Shark, Adventures of Gabriel Gale.*

34. Pius XII, Address to a Congress of the Latin Union of High Fashion, November 8, 1957.

35. See, among many others, Rm 12:2 ("Be not conformed to this world; but be reformed in the newness of your mind, that you may prove what is the good, and the acceptable, and the perfect will of God"); 1 Th 4:3-5 ("this is the will of God, your sanctification; that you should abstain from fornication; that every one of you should know how to possess his vessel in sanctification and honour: not in the passion of lust, like the Gentiles that know not God"); 1 Cor 5:9-13 ("I have written to you, not to keep company, if any man that is named a brother, be a fornicator, or covetous, or a server of idols, or a railer, or a drunkard, or an extortioner: with such a one, not so much as to eat").

36. Pope Pius XII, Allocution to Catholic Girls, 22 May 1941.

37. In case you're not familiar with this expression, a Mother Hubbard Dress refers to a long, wide, loose-fitting gown with long sleeves and a high neck, that was popular in some places in the 19th century.

38. Fr Stefano Manelli, Fr., FFI, *Jesus Our Eucharistic Love*, p. 67. Valatie, NY: The Academy of the Immaculate, 1996.

39. Dorothy M. Gaudiose, *Prophet of the People*, pp. 191-2. Staten Island, NY: Alba House Publishers, 1988.

40. Pope Pius XII, Address to a Congress of the Latin Union of High Fashion, November 8, 1957. The pontiff added with his accustomed insight: "It can certainly be conceded that there are different degrees of public morality according to the times, the nature, and the conditions of the civilisation of individual peoples. But this does not invalidate the obligation to strive for the ideal of perfection and is not a sufficient reason to renounce the high degree of morality that has been achieved, and which manifests itself precisely in the great sensitivity with which consciences regard evil and its snares".

41. Cf. Anne Maloney, "What the Hookup Culture Has Done to Women", Crisis Magazine, June 2016, https://crisismagazine.com/opinion/hook-culture-done-women

42. Cf. St Teresa of Avila, *Life*, chapter 2.

43. Proverbs 31:30.

44. Cf. Gen 3:21.

45. Exhortation to Those In Authority Regarding Immodest Fashions in Women's Dress, Letter Issued from the Sacred Congregation of the Council by order of Pope Pius XI January 12, 1930. The full text of this exhortation can be found here: https://svbmv.files.wordpress.com/2012/10/1930-letter-of-the-congregation-of-the-council.pdf

46. *Summa Theologiæ*, IIa IIae, Q. 26, a. 5, see also Q. 169, a. 2

47. Cf. "On a pedestal: High heels and the perceived attractiveness and evolutionary fitness of women", https://www.sciencedirect.com/science/article/pii/S0191886921008357#bb0130; "High heels as supernormal stimuli: How wearing high heels affects judgements of female attractiveness", https://www.sciencedirect.com/science/article/pii/S1090513812001225.

48. The proper name for this procedure is "Breast/Buttock Augmentation with Fat Grafting", and it consists of fat transfer and implants. Fat is taken from one part of the body and injected into another; silicone implants are placed in the muscle layer to increase curvature.

    According to the annual statistics of the American Society of Plastic Surgery (FY 2019), buttock augmentation has increased by 90.3%, ranking 6th in the number of all plastic surgery procedures https://www.ncbi.nlm.nih.gov/pmc/articles/PMC10229674/

    "The buttocks are the centre of the posterior body and play a very important role in its contour. The buttocks play the same role as the breasts do on the front of a woman". https://www.australiaplasticsurgery.com.au/procedures/buttocks-enlargement-buttock-fat-injection-buttock-implants/

49. *Summa Theologiæ*, IIa-IIae, 169, 2, ad 1.

50. "It is one thing to counterfeit a beauty one has not, and another to hide a disfigurement arising from some cause such as sickness or the like. For this is lawful, since according to the Apostle (1 Cor. 12:23), 'such as we think to be the less honourable members of the body, about these we put more abundant honour'" (St Thomas Aquinas, *Summa Theologiæ*, IIa-IIae, 169, 2, ad 2).

51. *Summa Theologiæ*, IIa-IIae, 169, a. 2.

52. St Augustine, *Confessions*, Book 10.

53. Cf. J.M. Townsend and T. Wasserman, The Perception of Sexual Attractiveness: Sex Differences in Variability. Arch Sex Behav 26, 243–268 (1997). https://doi.org/10.1023/A:1024570814293: "Men's assessments of sexual attractiveness are determined more by objectively assessable physical attributes; women's assessments are more influenced by perceived ability and willingness to invest (e.g., partners' social status, potential interest in them)".
    N.B. There are numerous other recent studies and journal articles that prove this objectively. They have not been listed here due to the sometimes indelicate nature of the content.

54. For anyone who may seek further confirmation of what I write here, it may be helpful to know that over a century ago a group of researchers studied the functioning of human perception within the broader study of the human mind and behaviour as a whole. Their research led to a number of principles which came to be known as the Gestalt Principles, from the German word Gestalt, which can be translated as "a unified whole, or a configuration". The main principle evoked here is the Principle of Continuity. Cf. for example, Grace Fussell, Gestalt Theory: 6 Essential Principles for Design, https://www.shutterstock.com/blog/gestalt-theory-in-design. See also Stylumia, Good To Great Designs: Gestalt Principles, https://www.stylumia.ai/blog/good-to-great-designs-gestalt-principles/, and Guide to the Gestalt Principles: Role of Gestalt Laws in Design, https://www.masterclass.com/articles/gestalt-principles-guide.

The Gestalt Principles, even though rather recently classified and formulated, are not new; they simply explain what we can observe ourselves. People involved in advertising and fashions know these principles well and have made abundant use of them; they go a long way towards explaining why the increased sexualisation of our society has gone hand in hand with more and more daring fashions that reveal both the flesh and the form of the female body.

55. Cf. Notification Concerning Men's Dress Worn by Women, 12 June 1960.

56. Pius XII, Allocution to the Girls of Catholic Action, May 22, 1941.

57. Gerard J. M. Van Den Aardweg, *The Battle for Normality: A Guide For (Self-) Therapy For Homosexuality*, p. 78 and ff.. San Francisco: Ignatius Press, 1997.

58. St Thomas explains that "it is in itself sinful for a woman to wear man's clothes, or vice versa; especially since this may be a cause of sensuous pleasure; and it is expressly forbidden in the Law (Dt. 22) because the Gentiles used to practice this change of attire for the purpose of idolatrous superstition. Nevertheless this may be done sometimes without sin on account of some necessity, either in order to hide oneself from enemies, or through lack of other clothes, or for some similar motive" (*Summa Theologiæ,* Ia-IIae, 169, a. 2, ad 3).

59. I do hold that it is unbecoming for women to engage in certain sports (e.g. boxing, wrestling, weight lifting,..), not for any lack of capacity, but for reasons of feminine dignity and decorum.

60. Isaiah 47:2-3.

61. Exhortation to Those in Authority Regarding Immodest Fashions in Women's Dress, Letter Issued from the Sacred Congregation of the Council by order of Pope Pius XI January 12, 1930; Pope Pius XI, Encyclical *Divini illius magistri*, "On The Christian Education of Youth," 31 December 1929. Cf. also Pope Pius XII, July 17, 1954: "Do they not see the harm resulting from excess in certain gymnastic exercises and sports not suitable for virtuous girls?".

62. Here again we can refer to the Gestalt Principles, namely the Principle of Focal Point, which confirms what is here explained from a psychological point of view.

63. Study led by psychologist Susan Fiske. A summary can be found here: https://www.nationalgeographic.com/science/article/bikinis-women-men-objects-science. The full study can be found here: https://www.ncbi.nlm.nih.gov/pmc/articles/PMC3801174/

64. It has further been noticed by researchers that when the male gaze is drawn to a woman's face, it is geared towards finding a potential long-term spouse, whereas when it is drawn to her bodily features, he pays less attention to the face and is drawn to short term gratification. "Not only are males more likely than females to state a preference for physically attractive characteristics in a mate, but their prioritizing of female facial cues over body shape is dependent on the planned mating duration. That is, whereas females remain unaffected by mating temporality, males prioritize facial cues in a long-term mating context but

bodily cues in a short-term one." https://www.ncbi.nlm.nih.gov/pmc/articles/PMC8133465/

65. Cf. https://www.history.com/this-day-in-history/bikini-introduced.

66. For modest swimming apparel, try this: https://www.etsy.com/au/market/modest_swimsuit, or this: https://calypsa.com/swimwear.html, or this: https://www.modestmermaid.co/

67. Pope Pius XII, through delegation to Cardinal Pietro Ciriaci, Prefect of the Sacred Congregation of the Council, August 15, 1954.

68. *Summa Theologiæ*, Ia-IIae, 109, 8, corpus.

69. Quote attributed to Edmund Burke (1729-1797).

70. *The Visions of Saint Frances of Rome: Hell, Purgatory, and Heaven Revealed* (p. 59). TAN Books. Kindle Edition.

APPENDIX

Practical Points
on Modesty for Men and Women

> I want women to adorn themselves with proper clothing, modestly and discreetly.
>
> *1 Timothy 2:9*

PRELIMINARY CONSIDERATION

In order to safeguard the dignity of your person, when dressing ask yourself what is the best way to cover your body, that is, your skin but also your shape. If you find yourself wondering how to reveal parts of the body or show its form, then you are not dressing but undressing. Furthermore, if you find yourself constantly adjusting your clothing to ensure coverage, it is certainly not appropriate.

STANDARDS FOR WOMEN

Always ensure:

- Appropriate coverage of the upper body (bodice, abdomen, chest, shoulders, back) with an appropriate neckline (2 fingers breadth below the neck at most).

- Sleeves on all garments, ideally to the elbow but at the very least quarter length.

- Appropriate hem lines. When seated, your hem line should go well past your knees to ensure full coverage of knees in all positions without having to pull or stretch the skirt. Appropriate undergarments. A petticoat or slip that conceals underwear and shape as much as possible. (Unless the dress is of thick, coarse material, men do not fail to notice if a woman is not wearing proper underclothes).

Always avoid:

- Tight-fitting clothes, especially leggings and tight-fitting shirts or sweaters. All of these highlight in an inappropriate way the female form.
- Transparent fabrics (unless over sufficiently solid material to conceal the flesh).
- Flesh-coloured fabrics (it gives the illusion of no clothes).
- Low-cut tops or blouses.
- Loose necklines that can be revealing when bending over.
- Clothing with advertising or slogans especially on the chest area (as it draws the eye).
- Trousers (unless in one of the situations mentioned in letter 3). Leggings are never modest unless under a skirt of normal length.
- Shorts.
- Slits in skirts or dresses. Remember Isaiah 47 which equates bare legs and shoulders with shame.

Swimwear
(as per guidelines detailed in letter 4)

- https://www.etsy.com/au/market/modest_swimsuit
- https://calypsa.com/swimwear.html
- https://www.modestmermaid.co/

STANDARDS FOR MEN

Although the Church has not provided a universal standard for men's clothing, still, some guidelines can be found. In May 1946 the Canadian Bishops directed these words on modesty to men: "Man himself does not escape from the inclination of exhibiting his flesh: some go in public, stripped to the waist, or in very tight trousers or in very scanty bathing suits. They thus commit offences against the virtue of modesty. They may also be an occasion of sin (in thought or desire) for our neighbour." What would seem to be the more urgent problem in regard to men's dress is the fact that it has become overly casual, even in church. The ideal form of dress for men in most contexts is loose fitting shirts and slacks. Long, loose fitting shorts are acceptable for sports, hiking and certain types of work. Casual clothes and shirts with slogans should not be worn in church. Consequently the following are to be ruled out:

- Tight trousers and shorts.
- Short shorts.
- Low-cut trousers that expose undergarments.
- Muscle shirts.
- Singlets.
- Low-buttoned shirts.
- Being shirtless.
- Overly casual clothes except for casual events (*never* in church).
- Immodest bathing suits (speedos50).
- Earrings and other marks of effeminacy.
- T-shirts or jumpers with large slogans or pictures.

MODESTY IN CHURCH

> **THE CHURCH IS THE HOUSE OF GOD.**
>
> IT IS FORBIDDEN FOR MEN TO ENTER WITH
> BARE ARMS OR IN SHORTS.
>
> IT IS FORBIDDEN FOR WOMEN TO ENTER IN TROUSERS,
> WITHOUT A VEIL ON THEIR HEAD, IN SHORT CLOTHING,
> LOW NECKLINES, SLEEVELESS OR IMMODEST DRESSES

Words from a sign on the door of the church in San Giovanni Rotondo, Italy, in the days of St Pio of Pietrelcina, circa 1960.

- Keep within the modesty guidelines for daily dress.
- Put on your best to go to Sunday Mass.
- Clothing should not be ostentatious or distracting.
- If you go to church during the week, wear clothes that are not casual, but worthy of God's house.
- Men should uncover their heads prior to entering a church (even when the Blessed Sacrament is not present).
- Women should cover their heads prior to entering a church (even when the Blessed Sacrament is not present).

A FINAL THOUGHT

An Admonition Against Vanity from
St Frances of Rome

In the life of Saint Frances of Rome (1384-1440), we read that God showed her, among her many visions of the fires of Hell, the souls of certain ladies whom she had known in Roman society, "who had been excessively captivated by vanity and concern for the cultivation of physical beauty". They had sought to "increase their ability to captivate men, and... to enhance their looks in a deceptive manner".

For following the fashion of the day in indecent styles of dress, they became a cause of seduction and sin, and were now plunged for all eternity into the infernal torments.

This vision of Hell so marked Saint Frances of Rome, that she had it painted on the murals of her chapel, as a constant reminder of the judgments of God.[70]

About the Author

Dom Pius Mary Noonan is a Benedictine Monk and Priest. Born in Kentucky (USA), he became a professed monk at Abbaye Saint Joseph in Flavigny-sur-Ozerain (France). Since 2017 he has been the Prior of a Benedictine Foundation called Notre Dame Priory in Colebrook, Tasmania. Dom Pius holds a doctorate in Sacred Theology from the Institut Saint Thomas d'Aquin (Institut Catholique of Toulouse, France), and before leaving France was Director of Studies at the Abbey of Flavigny. As part of his community's apostolate, Dom Pius conducts spiritual retreats in various places around Australia and in the United States.

Other Works By Dom Pius Mary Noonan

The Grace to Desire It
St Benedict, the Father of Western Monks, teaches that there are Twelve Degrees or Steps of Humility. This little book explores each of these steps, prayerfully seeking out their meaning and proposing practical ways in which they can be reached and lived out in day to day life.

Whilst It Is Day

Life is short. At the very moment of our death, we are judged according to the way we lived. In this book, Dom Pius Mary Noonan shows that it is a divinely revealed truth that the limited time of this life is given to us in order to choose God and save our soul, and that when the hour of death has come, our fate is decided. There are no second chances after death, so we must be prepared now to meet our Maker. The best way to have a happy life is to be prepared at all times for a holy death.

Divine Providence and Human Freedom

St Paul tells us that "for those who love God, all things work together unto good" (Rm 8:28). If this is so, then God is secretly at work in every event of our lives, guiding all things to their eternal goal. In that grand scheme of things, we have our role to play. By doing good we further the plans of Divine Providence, we become His co-workers. This book, which seeks to delve into this mystery, will change your life and give you renewed incentive to become a saint.

To order these titles or to see more of the titles published by Cana Press go to: https://www.notredamemonastery.org/product-category/cana-press/. All titles are available on Amazon and other major book sellers or ask your local bookstore to order in a copy from their distributor.

www.ingramcontent.com/pod-product-compliance
Lightning Source LLC
Chambersburg PA
CBHW031421290426
44110CB00011B/478